Mary Ward

MARY WARD

1585-1645

"That incomparable woman."—*Pius XII*

by Mary Oliver, I.B.V.M.

Introduction and Epilogue

by *Maisie Ward*

SHEED AND WARD — NEW YORK

Acknowledgement

We thank Oxford University Press for permission to reprint passages from *The Poems of Gerard Manley Hopkins* (New York and London, 1937).

Note

Where the documentary sources of this book give a mere statement of fact, the author has set the facts against the cultural background of the day, giving imaginative details occasionally to fill in the picture. Some of the conversations are imaginatively reconstructed, but the words put into Mary's mouth are her own.

The biography follows closely the admirable two-volume work (now out of print) of Mother Catherine Chambers, I.B.V.M., with its long, sympathetic introduction by the Reverend H. J. Coleridge, S.J., written in 1802. Mother Chambers incorporates most of Mary's own autobiography and the biography written by Winefrid Wigmore, Mary's daughter and close friend.

Throughout this biography there are references to certain pictures, chosen from the series called *The Painted Life of Mary Ward*. The originals (fifty of them) are in the convent of the Institute of the Blessed Virgin Mary, Augsburg. They were painted in the seventeenth century.

Contents

When we read the words of Pius XII we marvel that Mary Ward should have had to suffer so much to set on foot much that is to us a matter of course: not even a Secular Institute with some freedom for future adaptations, but just a religious order without enclosure, governed not by the local bishop but by a Mother General directly under Rome.

We must set the story in the framework of history, and then we may begin to understand. As far as the universal Church was concerned, Mary, in asking for no enclosure, was going dead against the trend of the times, which, especially since the Council of Trent, was for more, not less, seclusion for all nuns. St. Teresa's reforms against worldliness made the strictest enclosure a chief element. Active orders of women were in their infancy, and the Ursulines, beginning without it, asked for a bull of enclosure from Paul V in 1612; so, three years later, did the new order of Notre Dame. When St. Francis de Sales, an eminent bishop, sought to establish for the Visitation a Rule with much-modified enclosure, he found so deep-rooted an opposition that he gave up the idea. St. Vincent de Paul found that, since enclosure was literally impossible for his sisters, whose chief work was nursing the sick poor in their own homes, the only alternative was to give up the claim to be a religious order at all.

Almost as difficult was the question of government. Back in the first centuries of religious life we find in the East a struggle between the bishops and the (often unruly) monks and hermits who peopled the deserts of Egypt and Syria. A little later in the West St. Gregory the Great, himself a monk and sympathetic with monastic autonomy, carefully delimited the authority of bishop and abbot. As for women, while for many years in Church history we find abbesses with as much

authority as abbots—indeed St. Brigid of Ireland, St. Hilda of
Whitby, St. Bridget of Sweden ruled men as well as women—
such a thing would have been unthinkable in the Counter-
reformation period. Nuns were often in spiritual matters subject to the monks of the same order; for their external works
they were directly under the local bishop. When Clement XI
in 1703 uttered the famous words "Lasciate governare le donne
dalle donne" (let women be ruled by women), he was confirming a revolutionary change which today has become an
established custom.

If bishops are occasionally jealous of their authority, how
much more so were lesser men in their periods of high rule
of those they were pleased to call "the weaker sex." The phrase
"they are but women" which moved Mary Ward to wrath
was spoken often enough in the days of male supremacy, and
women's powers were very generally depreciated. Mary had
far less chance than St. Francis or St. Vincent of achieving her
goal.

All this was in Catholic countries: how much worse was the
situation in England. Mary was born while Elizabeth reigned,
but most of her active life was spent under the Stuarts. English
Catholics had clung to the Faith, suffering much with immense
courage; the advent of James, son of the Catholic Mary Queen
of Scots, had promised relief, the disappointment was acute,
the disillusionment bitter. And, as so often happens, the unity
of the persecuted minority was beginning to show cracks,
especially in an increasing cleavage between the secular clergy
and the religious orders—above all, the Jesuits, an order not
yet quite a hundred years old, whose founder was not yet
canonized. It was the Jesuit Rule, adapted for women, that
Mary believed herself inspired to take, and she and her little

band incurred in the eyes of the secular clergy all the odium of the order. "The Jesuitrices here follow their suit underhanded," wrote an English priest from Rome. "The Jesuits disclaim openly, but I know they assist underhand what they can."

Unfortunately this was very far from being the case. There was never any question in Mary's mind of her Institute being a branch of the Jesuits. She wanted the Rule and the name, but not, she said, "the dependency." And although some of her best friends and supporters were Jesuits, the General was most of the time in opposition, and the greater part of the order felt that Mary complicated their already difficult position and were eager to disclaim her, some even to persecute her. While Father Gerard, S.J., thought and wrote of her as a great servant of God, it was the head of the Jesuit house at Munich of whom Mary wrote from her prison: "Father Contzen makes braggs that he hath done this deed." The British ambassador at Brussels wrote to James I about "certain brainsick English gentlewomen at St. Omer." Among Catholics they were spoken of as "this exorbitant institute of women," as "gallopping girls"—from their frequent journeys—as "apostolical viragoes," and "notable goshops"; they were said to be no better than they should be, "gadding about," yet claiming the name of nun. They were "dangerous to other monasteries," seizing upon all who came from England for their own institute.

Even for their principal work of education, enclosure would in England itself have been totally impossible. Once they were recognized as nuns, flight would have been the only alternative to imprisonment or even death. As it was, wearing lay clothes, working as laywomen, several of them including Mary herself underwent periods of imprisonment. And it seems clear that while education was their primary work Mary did not think of it as the exclusive occupation of her remarkable regiment in the Church's army. A fascinating letter from a Sister Dorothea shows her filling a vital need in the desolate English countryside of the period. She is reporting to Mary, and we can imagine her letters read aloud at recreation in the communities "overseas."

We are reminded today of something that probably passed unnoticed by them: the gulf between the wealthy-educated and the poor-uneducated was as wide at that date as the gulf between men on the one hand and women and children on the other. All these were ranked together as "women, children and the lower sort."

"I dare not keep schools publicly [writes Dorothea] as we do beyond the seas . . . but I teach and instruct children in the houses of parents . . . and by that occasion I get acquaintance and, so gaining first the affections of their parents, after, with more facility their souls are converted to God. . . .

"Besides teaching of children, I endeavour to instruct the simple and vulgar sort, I teach them their *Pater*, *Ave*, Creed, Commandments, etc. . . . I tend and serve poor people in their sickness. I make salves to cure their sores, and endeavour to make peace between those at variance."

But, alas, when those who had ceased to be "living members of the Catholick Church . . . desire nothing more than to save their souls by means of the sacraments it is incredible to say how hard it is to find a priest to reconcile them; partly thro' the scarcity of priests, and partly through the fears of those with whom they live. . . . Three things I observe to happen at the conversion of any (1) That I never gain one alone, but more. (2) One at least ever dieth, the rest lives. (3) That whensoever any are reconciled presently comes upon us persecution much more vehement than at other times."

Often Dorothea walked many miles to find a priest for the dying, or for the many Catholics who from fear, lack of instruction or mere inability to practise, had lapsed from the Faith. At the risk both of his life and her own, she would arrange a meeting in a field between priest and penitent if no house were available. One of these priests, she related with some amusement, praising her warmly said it was a pity Mrs. Ward and her girls were not like Dorothea!

For wherever Mary or her Institute became known they were admired. The stories against them always arrived from some other town or country through the grape-vine of gossip initiated by her foes.

As time went on, the strain of the atmosphere affected some of "Mrs. Ward's girls" themselves. The vast majority were loyal to Mary, but not to know when or whether their Institute would be approved shook a few of them badly. Some were for changing the Rule, for going behind Mary's back to gain approbation for something less than she had asked. One lay-sister had her own "revelations" to set against Mary's, one of the older nuns left the Institute and furnished secret and libellous information to the English clergy which was made much use of in Rome. "What Pope," asked Fr. Gerard sadly, "would confirm a Religion [i.e. religious order] which is itself disunited?"

Seen in historical perspective, Mary becomes a figure of immense significance: a pioneer with all the loneliness that the word implies, the leader in that first brilliant and apparently unsuccessful engagement which so often initiates a triumphant campaign. Against her were arrayed not only bishops and secular clergy and Jesuits but all the force of custom, precedent and male supremacy, together with the weakness that an unconfirmed Rule was bound to engender. What had she on her side?

Only the greatness with which God had endowed her, which had grown with her steadfast co-operation, and the perfect trust in Him that never left her.

It is remarkable how different was the view of Mary taken by those who knew her only from rumours and those who had met her face to face. Ferdinand, Prince Bishop of Liége and Cologne, went so far as to compare Queen Elizabeth and Mary Ward in England to Eve and Our Lady: "What a woman has destroyed, by a woman may be restored." Bishop Blaise of Liége supported her petition to Rome and remained her friend always. Cardinal Federigo Borromeo, St. Charles's nephew, and Father Domenico di Gesù, Maximilian, Elector of Bavaria, and his wife, were her warm admirers, Maximilian saying that "the English had been the first to teach his people their faith: they were now to teach them the manner of Christian living." The Bishop of Perugia came out to meet her singing the *Te Deum* and wearing his full regalia. The nuns at the Anger convent, preparing to receive her as a heretic, realized there had been some gigantic error. "This is a great servant of God," one of them said; "our house is happy at her setting foot in it." The four cardinals before whom she pleaded in Rome tried hard to find a way, owing to the impression made on them by Mary, and one of them, Cardinal Borgia, finally refused to deal any further in the matter, saying that Mary's enemies were so many and powerful he could not help her but would certainly do nothing to harm so holy a woman. The Jesuit General, Father Mutius Vitelleschi, despite the bombardment he was under from inside and outside the order, became personally friendly to Mary when she was in Rome. The Pope himself seems to have signed the decree for closing her houses with deep reluctance. The Inquisitor later set to spy on her wrote to Rome in enthusiastic terms of her great holiness. She bewitched them all, said her enemies.

Pondering over Mary's letters, her short autobiographies, the biography by Winefrid Wigmore, one of her first companions, and the other early lives based on the memories of that first generation, the word that springs to mind is magnanimity. "To labour through love," Mary says, "even unto death appeared to me easy, but fear with me made little impression." A chief horror she noted about venial sin was that it makes "our mind abject and disposition servile." Her efforts and achievements during the successful beginnings seemed so easy that she feared they were too little supernatural. "I cannot think it is a great matter to speak upon occasion with princes or to whomsoever, to effect or bring to pass whatever is necessary." It was for "recreation" that she visited the persecuting Archbishop of Canterbury, and she made imprisonment certain when "taken" at the port by producing her rosary and rebuking the judge. She seems to have feared in herself as imperfection what was the natural expression of magnanimity. "Because," she resolves, "I am inclined to affect and undergo more willingly such things as hath the title and outward appearance of excellency and greatness, I will henceforth endeavour to embrace and execute more simpler things with a particular love, devotion and diligence."

She feared nothing: imprisonment in England, imprisonment in Bavaria, a life of intense penance, first among the Poor
Clares, later, not under obedience but of her own steady voli-
tion, vast labours, which with her austerities bore heavily on an
always delicate constitution. Her journeys alone would have
killed many a stronger woman: the first expedition to Rome
was made on foot at an *average* of twenty miles a day for two
months. On one day the little group walked thirty-five miles:
a single horse allowing an occasional respite for each pilgrim.
Bad inns, bad food, short sleep meant nothing to Mary. From
her very girlhood she seems to have risen above the ordinary
trials that break so many in mind or body: her testing was on
a higher plane: her chief agony the difficulty first in knowing
what *was* God's will—"which *only, only* I desired"—and then
in getting that will accepted and carried out.

Magnanimity makes hard things easy. "Mirth," Mary would
say in the worst times, "is next to grace."

When a high ecclesiastic had laid out a large sum of money
to intercept her letters, her counter-move was to invoke a
special angel, begging him to take care that the letters should
arrive safely. This note of divine confidence and more than
good-humoured tolerance is always heard in the very hottest
days of conflict. It was said that it was better to be Mary's
enemy than her friend—she prayed more often for you. She
chose the nickname of "Jerusalem" for her foes, reminding her
children that this persecution was winning for them everlasting
glory. She reminded them constantly that even those "bent to
do what hurt they can . . . can do no more than God will
suffer them."

A holy old Benedictine who worked twenty-two years on
the English Mission, spending three of them in prison, saw

much of Mary in her last months and spoke of her having "a charity that rather laboured to excuse the faults committed against her than to think they needed forgiveness" and "a great riches wherewith to oblige everybody in the midst of real poverty," but above all "a continuall commerce with God as if there had been none living but they two."

Even seen through others' eyes, Mary praying is an experience and just now and then we have a word of her own suggesting a profound contemplation: "He held my heart, I could not work"; "I am not so much moved to pray as called to see."

It was, says our Benedictine, "as if she had not lived in sense but in faith of the things that appear not. But all this and what I can say is short of what I feale, believe and know beyond my expressions."

Mary Ward

1. Mary Ward's First Word

"The Lord is the keeper of little ones."
(PS. 114)

THE BABY in her mother's arms struggled to be free. She had lately learnt that she could push her legs into action with some effect, for she was fifteen months old. Straining against her mother's protecting arm, she looked down at the spaniel puppy leaping to reach her feet and plainly inviting her to come down to play on the lawn. Baby Mary Ward understood him very well, but her short memory did not serve to remind her that she was always knocked over by the mischievous spaniel. She would spend most of the playtime on her back, her small feet waving despairing gestures as she struggled to regain her poise. Now, in her mother's arms, she grunted and stiffened her legs —admirable tactics for adventurous babies. But her mother merely moved her position, telling her that Daddy was coming and—"See the pretty ladies!" Mary's only comments were the coos and goos of babyhood. Two ladies in riding habits came out of the house and down the terrace to the spot where their hostess was standing with her baby. The ladies touched Mary's soft pink cheeks with their gloved fingers, pausing a minute to chat with her mother before going forward to mount the horses which grooms were holding.

It was an exciting morning. Boys with hounds rushed across

the courtyard from the kennels, doing their part in assembling the hawking party as it gathered beyond the terrace at the side of Mulwith Manor. Dogs barked and grooms called to each other as they led the horses from the stables or walked them about to ease their restiveness. Presently the falconers gathered with hooded hawks and jingling bells; and the clear sunshine of early spring shone on the horses' glossy flanks. The last to join the party was their host, Marmaduke Ward. As the ladies and their escorts laughed and chatted, he paused to say good-bye to his wife and baby daughter. He looked very well in his dark green riding-suit, with cloak, and a felt hat turned up with a pheasant's feather, his long brown boots of undressed leather reaching above his knees, and his daggers shining in his leather belt. His chestnut mare, prancing daintily to show her impatience, whinnied softly to see him. Presently horses and riders turned their faces to the Yorkshire moors.

Ursula set her baby daughter down on the lawn. All was quiet, allowing a blackbird high up in an elm tree to fill the garden with its song. The baby heard it and smiled with delight, but her mother's answering smile was thoughtful in its tenderness. The hawking party would return in the evening— at least the few who were house guests would return; the near neighbours would go to their own homes. Night would close round them and anxiety would press on them once more.

For it was the year 1586, when no good Catholic home was safe from the visits of the pursuivants who were government servants paid to hunt priests and those who allowed a priest to say Mass in their homes. There were no longer any Catholic churches in England. Those were the days when being a Catholic meant living dangerously and heroically. Not two months before, Margaret Clitheroe had been brutally put to death in York for giving shelter to priests, one of them being Francis Ingleby, Ursula Ward's cousin. He too was now suffering in York gaol, awaiting his martyrdom by execution.

Well might Ursula Ward look thoughtful, for one of her guests was a priest hiding at Mulwith Manor for a few days. Until that morning the Wards and their Catholic neighbours had lived for months without Mass. The night before, this hunted priest had arrived and heard confessions until late into the night. He had given them Holy Communion at Mass that morning. Now he was out on the moors with a falcon on his wrist. Dressed in secular clothes and one in a hawking party, he was safe at least for today.

After a little coaxing, baby daughter agreed to go inside with her mother, who felt she must see to her household. Servants were preparing the supper that was to be ready in the evening on the return of the hunters. Ursula Ward was a careful mistress and a gracious hostess, one of those valiant English women who kept their home life serene and sweet, providing the little joys of a normal life in spite of the terrors of persecution. Setting her baby on her feet in the nursery sitting-room where two maids were folding linen, the mother passed out to the buttery and dairy. Baby explored under a few chairs, tested the arm of one with her six teeth, was testing the edge of a table—still with the same teeth, excellent testers—when she suddenly saw the open window. With an excited little run Mary tottered towards it, just as her mother re-entered the room. Seeing the baby running towards the danger and beyond her grasp, the mother cried: "O Jesus, bless my child!" At her mother's voice Mary turned and came towards her, smiling her endearing smile as she said clearly: "Jesus." That was Mary Ward's first word. With her baby lips she had unconsciously proclaimed the eternal allegiance of her heart.

2. Riding with Father

"Lovely and secret as a child."
(RUPERT BROOKE)

As MARY laboriously threaded her needle her thoughts flew from the sampler on her knees to the new royal-blue riding habit she was to wear today for the first time. She would wear her hat with its curling feather. Already she could smell the special smell of her pony's coat. Father would be with her on his tall chestnut. She was glad all the riding lessons were over and that she was now allowed to manage the pony for herself without any guiding rein in Father's hand. When you are five you ought to be allowed to look after yourself. . . . The needle threaded, she began to poke it recklessly into the squares. A knot! But she would pat that out of sight—keep it on the under side. Trying to flatten out the woolly lump, she felt less sure of herself. Mother was to examine the stitches, and Mother had keen eyes. A little more slowly now. Steady! How stitches liked to go crooked. . . . Oh, Father would be here soon and she wouldn't be ready. More speed . . . more knots. With a kind of quiet desperation she cut the wool at the end of a row and showed the sampler to her mother, while her lively dark eyes rested doubtfully yet hopefully on her mother's face. She would not break her little daughter's high spirits but she must train her. "That is not well done, dear," she said quietly, and Mary, blinking to keep back her tears,

7

took the work and picked out the crooked stitches. But no sign of temper, for her mother had taught her the sweet reasonableness of self-control.

Soon the task was over, and with Mother's help she was dressed in her new—her first—riding habit. Pressing her smart little hat down on her dark wavy hair, she looked round for her gloves; then, taking her silver-topped riding whip from a drawer, she stood ready for Father. In sudden gratitude she put her arms round her mother's neck and kissed her face, so close to her own as her mother knelt beside her to adjust the folds of her habit. Then they went out hand-in-hand to the terrace to wait for her father, who had been occupied for an hour or so superintending the feeding of the poor men who called in dozens every day to the kitchen of Mulwith Manor. Now that there were no monasteries to give food to the poor and sick, the plight of these poor creatures was terrible. Deprived of their work on monastery lands, labourers roamed the roads as beggars. The Christian charity of such men as Marmaduke Ward made the only brightness in Elizabethan social history.[1]

Five-year-old Mary of course knew nothing of all this; but later she would help her father distribute food to the poor. Her young heart learned from her parents to love the poor and to treat them with respect. So now, knowing what delayed her father, she felt God would not be pleased with her if she grudged him to the poor men at the kitchen gate. Her mother and she enjoyed the autumn sunshine and the glowing colours of the shrubs in the garden. Out in the park beyond they could see the autumn glory of beeches and oaks, and Mary felt herself trembling with excitement at the thought of riding under

[1] See Appendix IA.

their canopy. At last her father arrived and the groom led the horses round from the stables. At the foot of the terrace father and daughter mounted and were soon out on the lane where the tall poplars in gold coats seemed to hold day-long ceremony. The riders turned to wave to Mother before putting their horses to a canter.

Back in the house Ursula Ward went to the nursery where the maid was preparing to take the two youngest children, Barbara and Elizabeth, for a walk. Their mother gave them her affectionate attention for a moment, but it was of the little rider in her royal-blue habit disappearing between the poplars that she was thinking. By turning her head that morning she could see in the uncertain candle-light the pale, steady face of her eldest daughter as she knelt upright and attentive all during Mass. Her mother had covered her eyes with her hands, trying to drive away anxious thoughts. At least she knew now what she must do. Her husband and she had talked long about their little five-year-old daughter, and had decided that she must go and stay for some time with her grandmother, Mrs. Wright, at Ploughland Hall. There were rumours that a fresh set of pursuivants were scouring Yorkshire for some priests lately come overseas from the English seminary at Rheims where they had been ordained. It was one of these priests, gay and young and daring, whom the Wards were now sheltering. The priest's hiding-hole in the library was in good order both at its entrance and exit,[2] and no priest had ever been found in their house. Still, it was dangerous living, and they had no wish to draw Mary into it, now that she was interested in the Mass and had begged to be allowed up in the chilly dawn to see the priest in his red vestments hold aloft the white Host. The child even

[2] See Appendix IB.

knew that two servants were keeping watch at windows in the lobby. Puzzling over too many things, she would be an embarrassing accomplice if questioned by pursuivants.

The way to the corn-fields ready for harvesting led Mary and her father through the outskirts of the village; but before they met anyone, Marmaduke Ward, with sudden resolution, dismounted, and under pretext of adjusting a buckle on Mary's bridle, stood close to her for a moment to say: "Darling, if we meet anyone, there will be no need for you to talk. Just answer with courtesy; that will be all anyone will expect from a little horsewoman only five years old." Everything her father did was just right, so Mary gave him an answering smile, saying cheerfully: "Yes, Father." Her father was hardly remounted when a solitary horseman rode out of a side street. It was the Protestant minister in charge of what used to be the Catholic church of the village. Her father and the horseman drew rein for a few minutes to exchange remarks about the good weather and the prospects of the harvest. The clergyman said he had not known Sir Marmaduke's daughter was old enough to manage her pony alone. Mary smiled but was obediently silent. . . . Relief and pain swept over her father's heart at the thought of her departure on the morrow.

As for the parson, studious and tolerant as he was, he must have ridden on his way wondering at the loyal adherence of Marmaduke Ward to the Old Faith. He himself had been born and educated a Protestant, but the memory of his fellow-student of Oxford days, Edmund Campion, had made him gentle towards Catholics. Campion's martyrdom in London nine years before had horrified him. And now, beyond reporting each month, as he was bound to do, that Marmaduke Ward had not taken Communion in the Church of England, he closed his eyes to anything that might be going on at Mulwith Manor. It would have been a triumph for the new religion in Yorkshire if the Wards and their relatives could be induced to take the Oath of Supremacy—the oath that made a Protestant out of a Catholic. Year by year all over England there were landowners, tired of paying recusancy fines, who, after holding out bravely for years, yielded and went to the Protestant church.

It was of these people that Marmaduke Ward was thinking as he rode on with Mary through the manor lands of Mulwith. He wondered how they could bring themselves to give up the Holy Mass and the sacraments. Yet his charity covered them, for he knew how every day and all day his heart was crying to God for strength and courage to be true to his faith. The heavy fines several times a year were a big strain. He had two other estates besides Mulwith—one at Newby, the other at Givendale. Knowing the greed of the new aristocracy that were thriving on stolen money and lands, he felt pretty sure that he would not be imprisoned while he could furnish big sums of money in recusancy fines. He would eventually have to sell one of his estates. God grant that it be not too soon. What would become of his Catholic tenants and workmen if they were dependent on some bitter master climbing steadily in the Queen's favour? No. He would try to manage by selling a field just now and again. These were heavy thoughts, but being a Catholic in Elizabethan times gave men practice in heroism.

3. Ploughland

*"There pipes the woodlark, and the song-
thrush there
Scatters her loose notes in the waste of air."*
(GRAY)

AFTER HER first weeks of loneliness Mary settled down to the quiet, somewhat austere, routine of life at Ploughland, a manor house on what had once been a fine property in the East Riding of Yorkshire. For generations it had been in the hands of the Wrights, and Mary's mother had grown up in its heroic atmosphere—heroic, for it must have been sobering, to say the least, for a young girl to know that her mother was in prison suffering for her Catholic faith. Different periods of imprisonment added up to fourteen years in the life of Mary's grandmother. When Mary went to live with her she was middle-aged, sanctified by great suffering, but by no means broken in courage, for she risked her life constantly in sending food and clothing to prisoners, in paying recusancy fines for poorer Catholics, and in working for the education of priests abroad. Field after field she sold to obtain the money she needed, until, at the time of Mary's arrival in 1590, Ploughland was only a small holding. "Well done," would have been the approving comment of Grandmother's grandfather, Sir William Mallory, had he been alive. In the early days of the Protestant reformation, he had stood outside the village church with drawn sword, defying the government agents who tried to enter and wreck it. Mallory was a man of such standing in Yorkshire that the agents feared for their lives if they laid a finger on him. So Sir William won that round of the fight.

Ploughland was a well-built house standing on a wooded hill at a distance from the highway. It seemed a lonely place to Mary after the brightness of Mulwith. No hawking parties here, with brave knights and well-dressed ladies. No little sisters. And, worst of all, no young mother and father. But Mary's destiny needed the five years she was to spend at Ploughland. Her studies began early, and by the time she was nine years old she was able to speak fluently in Italian and to read Latin. Her grandmother had sent her in the summer of that year to spend some months with her cousins the Inglebys at Ripley Castle, for she felt that a change of air—not to speak of youthful companionship—was necessary for her lively grand-daughter. A young Protestant who later became a Catholic and a priest in Rome wrote: "Whilst I was at Ripley Castle a certain noble Catholic virgin [surely Mary?] had lately arrived, with whom I very frequently conversed on the Catholic faith, and who satisfactorily removed many doubts from my mind; and some others were postponed for the time, as she said she was going to her grandmother who lived near, in a day or two, who would remove every doubt from me. . . . On my departure the noble lady gave me a rosary, the Office of the Blessed Virgin, and the Psalter of Jesus." Very good for a nine-year-old apostle!

Several things had helped in the last four years to develop Mary Ward's personality, the first being the strong influence of her grandmother. Even when she was only six years old her grandmother had told her of the Catholics languishing in prison for their faith, and encouraged her to add her mite to the parcels prepared at Ploughland for them. Mary used to save up her pennies for the prisoners, and even gave her two little white hens that she had petted in the fowl-yard. When she asked her grandmother what made the dents on her ivory-handled walking stick, she was told that Grandmother had used the stick to keep off the rats when she—yes, Grandmother! —was in prison. The marks were left by the bites of the rats. Rats' teeth! And Mary shivered. Her grandmother told her of the confessors and martyrs all over England who went in danger of torture because they loved the Holy Mass and our Crucified Lord more than they loved anything on earth. And the Mass seemed to the little girl more beautiful and precious as each one passed. But how rare those Masses were. Occasionally word would travel round the countryside among the Catholics—but it had to travel very secretly indeed, for there were spies everywhere. And the message was: Mass will be celebrated at five (or perhaps, six) in the morning at such a house.

On one such morning Mass was to be said at five o'clock at Ploughland. Mary was only seven years old, but her grandmother gladly gave her permission to get up for Mass. Before Mary was out of bed she could see through her window signs of travellers coming up the hillside. Although it was early spring, it was quite dark when the first neighbours arrived. The priest had come during the night and was hearing confessions before Mass. Nearly all of those who came would be fasting, some having ridden through hilly country from about two o'clock. Up the hillside they came, silent men and women on horseback, each with a glowing lantern strapped to one stirrup.

Her grandmother came to Mary's bed to tell her to dress. Soon she was kneeling in the small parlour that had been fitted up as a chapel. A clear fire in the grate helped to light the room; the candles on the altar were the only other lights. The priest in his red vestments came through the doorway and Mass began. If he was found in this house, he would be taken to York or London and tortured before being put to death.

The priest held up the white Host. Silence and adoration; an occasional coal falling in the fireplace was the only sound. He raised the chalice with self-offering and a wordless cry of the heart for courage to face what might be ahead. Then everyone in the room went to receive Holy Communion— all except Mary. But her grandmother had taught her about the great graces that came to those who only desired to receive their Lord; so Mary bowed her little dark head in the strong prayer of desire. At every Mass she was growing in spiritual stature and in a dignity beyond her years.

Even at Ploughland evil could creep in, and Mary's own account tells quaintly of a "near kinswoman of mine whom God had endued with many gifts" which she made no good use of, who was also living there and had for attendant "a young gentlewoman, who though in show modest, yet was she indeed light of carriage." Mary was much attached to her young relative, about her own age and probably her aunt, and whenever possible spent her time with her. She lists contritely her childish crimes: "When my grandmother commanded me to pray, I sat in the place, but spent my time in sports. . . . In this five years my fortune was asked and told several times, once or twice I think I procured it. . . . according to my capacity I believed what was said." There were, too, some superstitious practices. One of these was to fast on St. Agnes Eve in the hope of seeing in a dream the person one would marry. But after a good part of the day, "being then very

hungry," says Mary, "I broke off." Then there was "the unlawful practice of sive [*sic*] and shears . . . for the finding
out of a trifle of mine that was lost." The points of the shears
were stuck into the wood of a sieve, and Saints Peter and Paul
invoked as to whether A, B, or C was the thief. On the right
name being uttered, the sieve would suddenly whirl round.

Suddenly, after one of their escapades, Mary experienced
such a revulsion of feeling that she ran to her room and, on her
knees, asked Our Lord to pardon her for turning away from
His love. That night as she awoke from sleep the rain was
pouring on the roof, the wind lashing the trees in the garden.
The little girl in bed felt a strange feeling of comfort, like one
who has come safely home. Over in the darkest corner of the
room on her *prie-dieu* knelt the valiant grandmother. "So
great a prayer was she," Mary says, that sharing her bedroom:
"I do not remember in that whole five years that I ever saw
her asleep, nor did I ever wake, when I perceived her not at
prayer." Mary realized with a feeling of tenderness that these
prayers had kept her safe. In the autobiography she writes, "O
my God, in what state had I now been, if You had not done
all!"

4. Back at Mulwith

"When drop-of-blood-and-foam-dapple
Bloom lights the orchard apple"
(GERARD MANLEY HOPKINS)

AT TEN years of age Mary was a tall graceful girl, and when
we recall the customs of the Middle Ages and of Tudor England we need not be surprised to hear that before her eleventh
year a marriage was arranged for her. The suitor was a boy
named Redshaw whose father asked Mary's father for leave
to make the offer. In such cases it was understood that the
young pair, though betrothed, would not marry for a few
years. In the seventeenth-century *Painted Life* of Mary we
see the boy's formal request and her dignified acceptance. We
have to take the artist's word that she is accepting; for that
prim little figure might be saying anything. In the right panel
of the picture she is with her parents and her sister Teresa.
She is more animated here, and we feel she is glad to be giving
pleasure to her parents.

An early biography based on that of Winefrid Wigmore,
close friend and confidante of Mary, relates quaintly Mary's
own feelings and the end of the story: "God whose works are
ever admirable, weaned her from this beginning of love, by
an apprehension of some lack of constancy and fervour in her
pretended spouse his respects to herself, which yet really was
not so, for he both loved and honoured her till his death, which
in a few months after happened."

By this date, 1594, Mary was back home again, and lessons and long rides with her father made the days seem short. The family circle had grown while she was at Ploughland; besides Barbara and Elizabeth there were now Teresa and the little brothers, John and George. When the long summer evenings lingered round the manor, she would play with her brothers and sisters in the garden, hiding behind the shrubs and romping on the lawn. . . .

One evening it was time to go to bed. They had prepared for bed in the nursery, but Mary had to go upstairs to her own room. She told the maid she was too tired to walk upstairs. The maid smiled as she said breezily, "I'll carry you, Miss Mary," and she was mounting the stairs when, adjusting her burden, she lost her balance, slipped and let the child fall headlong.

In her room Mary lay stunned and speechless but conscious. The family gathered round her in fear and grief, thinking she was about to die. Till the end of her life she remembered lying there, thinking in her heart: "If only I could say the holy name of Jesus I would gladly die." Summoning her powers, she murmured: "Jesus." And with that word of salvation, joy and sweetness came into her soul. All pain and distress passed, and her loved ones knew she was resting in a healing sleep.

Summer cooled into autumn, and fires were lit in the manor house. Mary loved the long evenings after supper when, while all the other children were asleep upstairs, she sat in the little blue wainscoted parlour where the fire burned with a deliciously resinous smell as the pine logs, still on the green side,

gave body and heat to the dry wood. Candles in silver candle-
sticks lighted the room, and Mary worked at her embroidery
near a little table by the fire while her father read, often in
French and Italian (for the old aristocracy in Renaissance England loved literature and languages). Very often a priest to
whom they were giving shelter would be an honoured guest.
He would talk to them about his life at Rheims and of his
return to England, where spies had set plots to catch him.
Nothing seemed to daunt these young English priests. Their
numbers in 1585 had been one hundred. And now there were
five hundred of them, hunted and harried as if they were wild
beasts. As she sat there, Mary's thoughts would go to all the
priests she had seen saying Mass at Ploughland; and she would
think of them as they laid their hands in blessing on her head
(for her grandmother always took her to the priest that he
might bless her before he went out again into danger). Then
Mary would recall her thoughts to the grave voice of the young
priest sitting by her own home fire. Tomorrow he would say
Mass in the hush of the dawn on the altar that she would prepare with her mother. Servants would take turns in watching
for the pursuivants that might even now be preparing to raid
this peaceful home. If they came, her father would smuggle
the priest into the hiding-hole built specially behind a secret
panel for hunted priests. She had seen this happen once when
the dogs had barked and a false alarm was given. She would
look across at the young priest, so lately ordained—ordained,
very probably, for martyrdom. Encounters with such bravery
awakened in Mary a desire to be used wholly for God's glory.
Already she was taking her heroic, suffering countrymen into
the harbour of her heart.

One day not very long after Mary's return home she was standing with two of her sisters at a window looking out over the park. The snows had melted, but the cold winds from the moors were tossing the bare limbs of the trees: occasionally, with a great crash, one would fall to their buffeting. The room where the children were playing was in a remote wing of the house; they often went to dress up in old-fashioned clothes from the trunks stored there. As they looked out of the window they could see some of the men gathering up branches blown from the walnut trees. Suddenly the men came running towards the house, waving their hands. More men. Then shouts and the acrid smell of smoke. The house was on fire!

Mary ran to the door and opened it. Smoke was billowing up the corridor from the front of the house. Seizing the little sisters, she turned in the other direction where it seemed clear, down a short stairway to a room below. Even there the smoke was rolling towards them. Had she been alone, Mary might have made a dash for safety. But her good angel warned her against trying to escape with the children. In the room was "a trunk or coffer filled with linen damask, which I had heard some say my mother laid apart for me; which coffer with the help of my sisters I drew into the chimney . . . and then we set ourselves to pray the Mother of God that she would not permit the house to be burnt."

Suddenly there was a shout—her father's voice, quite near. They ran to the door and shouted back. Out of the smoke dashed that loved form, torn, blackened and dishevelled—but, Father. Picking up the little girls in his arms, he told Mary to cling to him; and they raced down the corridor to safety. (The artist in the *Painted Life* must have tidied them all up, for they did not step so trimly from that burning building!)

The house was too badly burnt for repairs, so the family packed up and travelled some miles across the country to another property. Here they took over, from relatives, Marmaduke's fine mansion of Newby.

5. Mary's First Communion

*"Love Him and keep Him for thy friend
who, when all go away, will not leave thee."*
(À KEMPIS)

WHEREVER MOTHER and Father are, there is home, when we are young. So the children were delighted with everything at Newby Hall. The house was more spacious and the grounds more carefully planned than at Mulwith. As the cold winds of March gave way to the softness of spring, Mary and her brothers and sisters were out-of-doors all the sunlight hours until a schoolroom programme was drawn up for them. On the north of the Hall were the stables and kennels; on the south, the gardens that swept down to the wrought-iron gates standing between their posts of stone sculptured into the forms of lions. Until the children grew accustomed to this imposing gateway, they would stand well back from the lions, giving them stare for stare. At one side of the garden was a lake sheltered in part by weeping willows, clad in the early days of spring in a filmy green veil. No children had lived at the Hall for some years, and the birds and animals seemed to delight in the new spirit that six healthy children scattered as they ran. Even the swans on the lake would edge their fluffy cygnets up to the stone border for the children to admire as they scattered crumbs. Beyond the lake lay the park, and beyond that again untouched woodland, gay with wild daffodils, where the nightingales sang in the early morning. All this

beauty passed into Mary's being to become a poignant joy in
the years of exile.

Within the house itself everything was strongly built, a
great deal of its furnishings being of polished oak and brass.
Most of the rooms were lined with oak and had oaken floors,
covered here and there with rugs from Italy. Halfway up the
walls the oak panelling gave place to brightly worked tapestries. Upstairs, at the end of the gallery that faced the setting
sun, was a stained-glass window bearing the emblazoned coat
of arms of the Ward family. As Mary came down to supper
she used to be delighted by its shining beauty. The blue field
with the gold cross grew brilliant against the setting sun. When
Mary returned from supper the azure had grown sombre, but
the gold cross seemed to hold the evening light. In a few years
that would be an image of her life: the cross of suffering
touched by glory against the sombre field of daily duty. That
spring of 1596 was one of the few springtimes that Mary spent
at Newby Hall.

Beyond the home circle persecution was beginning one of
its raging seasons in Yorkshire. The discovery of the Babington Plot led to the execution of Anthony Babington, that
brilliant, restless man whose life was dedicated to the tragic destiny of Mary, Queen of Scots. Anthony Babington was well
known to Marmaduke Ward, who refused, however, to meddle in any way with politics; not all Anthony's enthusiasm
was able to move him. There were few of his friends who
could withstand Anthony's charm. That was why Marmaduke
Ward felt uneasy whenever this young man visited Yorkshire,
for Ursula Ward's brothers were only too ready to be caught
up in any conspiracy against Queen Elizabeth, whom they

considered a usurper. In their eyes Mary, Queen of Scots, was the rightful queen, and John and Christopher Wright were ready to lay down their lives for her. While Mary Ward's father hated the subversive talk of his brothers-in-law, they, on their side, were angered by his mild outlook; and, on the defeat of the Armada in 1588, his satisfaction at the defeat of the Spaniards had put his political-minded brothers-in-law out of all patience. . . . Poor Anthony Babington. He was only twenty-five when he was executed in September 1596.

It was probably to strike fear into any other possible Catholic conspirators that Elizabeth set going at full pace the barbarous machinery of the Penal Laws. One of her most willing agents was Lord Huntingdon, President of the North, with headquarters at York. He needed no urging, and in 1596 no less than eleven Catholics (most of them belonging to the landed gentry) were put to death in York prison. Reports came to Marmaduke Ward and his wife that Huntingdon was turning his attention to them. So, sadly, but with swift efficiency, Mary's mother and father packed as much as they considered necessary and set out with their family in the early hours of a dark morning for a long journey to Northumberland where, at Alnwick Castle, they were to be the guests of the newly-married Martha and her husband, Thomas Percy. Because of the harsher northern climate, Mary was not taken but left in the care of a cousin, Mrs. Ardington, who was a daughter of Sir William Ingleby of Ripley Castle.

But before the Wards left Newby a young Northumbrian gentleman asked for the hand of Mary in marriage. His name was Shafto, and everyone said that it would be a most advantageous alliance; but Mary would not even consider it. The inscription on this picture of the *Painted Life* tells us that she re-

fused her suitor with "great warmth." Young Mr. Shafto is
bearing up well, though behind that pleasant exterior he may
well be ruefully muttering: "Why didn't somebody tell me?"

Ardington was a fairly new house built of brick in the Elizabethan style, with a wide entrance porch in the middle on the
ground floor. Over the main entrance doors there were carved
pediments: also over the windows. Balustrades here and there
on the two upper storeys showed that the Renaissance style
of architecture had come to Elizabethan England. The garden
was laid out with great care in flower beds, lawns and shrubs
cleverly cut into shapes of birds and animals. This topiary
work in gardens was a feature of landscape gardening at this
era. Hedges of dwarf-height clipped yew bordered the paths,
and on the silent summer nights Mary loved to hear the fountain splashing softly into its stone basin. . . . It was here, in
the summer of 1598, that she made her First Holy Communion.
The date was arranged early in August, and it was set down
for the 8th of September, Our Lady's birthday. For a year or
more, the great day of her First Communion had been her
guiding thought, and as it approached she prepared with great
care, entering on an intensive preparation on the 15th of August, the feast of the Assumption. In this as in everything else
throughout her life she was to be Our Lady's special child; all
the more so as she was henceforth to live apart from her tender-
hearted parents—a great loss for a girl of twelve.

As the day of her First Communion drew near, Mary prayed
with deeper recollection and piety, withdrawing as much as
possible from the social life of the house. A few days before
the 8th of September, she was kneeling in the chapel before
supper one evening when one of the servants came to tell her

that there was a gentleman at the gate with a message from her father. Surprised with joy to hear of her father, Mary ran down the corridor and out to the garden at the back of the house. On the outside of the fence was a horseman who held a letter in his hand, saying he had been told by her father not to give it to her, but to read it to her. And there in the summer evening with the long shadows falling across the lawns, while a few bees were paying a last visit to the lavender walk, and the horse was jingling his bridle, Mary listened in deepest distress. Her father wished her not to make her First Communion, but to hold herself prepared to marry one of the Talbots of Grafton. Before she could ask a question the man had wheeled his horse and galloped into the twilight.

The artist of the *Painted Life* has shown it well in his primitive style. . . . In a moment Mary turned to go into the house, trying to hold her emotions in check until she reached her room. Never in her short life had she felt so lonely, and in her loneliness and bewilderment she wept tears beyond any childhood grief. Not to make her First Communion! And Mother and Father forcing her into marriage! . . . The supper bell rang, and, hastily bathing her eyes, she composed herself to meet the rest of the household in the dining-room. Asked about her tears, she would not tell her trouble to anyone. But when she went into the chapel "she seemed to feel a loving reproach from God Almighty for her ingratitude. She remained in this conflict till she resolved to communicate the first opportunity she should have."

Her father had of course sent no message, and assured her that he neither thought of keeping her back from Communion nor of marrying her against her will.

Mrs. Ardington's home was a centre for the Catholics living

in the adjacent districts. She had a resident chaplain who spent most of his time in the saddle, riding through that part of Yorkshire, instructing and encouraging his flock, staying no more than one night in a house lest he be a danger to these good people in remote districts. . . . Before he had set out on his journey from Harewell at the end of August, the priest blessed Mary, and asked her to pray for him, promising that he would return to give her First Holy Communion on the Feast of Our Lady's Nativity.

As the eve of the feast deepened into night and the priest had not returned, Mary had to summon all her faith and trust in God's providence. The neighbours, far and near, would be even now preparing to ride across country to the early morning Mass. In the chapel the altar was ready; and in Mary's own room her First Communion dress and veil were spread out. She had a moment of loneliness at the thought that her mother and father would not be there; but as she lay in bed she could recall their dear voices, and how her mother had once said that she must never feel lonely without them, for "God is the keeper of little ones." She closed her eyes and tried to sleep, but to her sharp hearing every tiny noise seemed to crack the silence of the night. The fountain, which usually splashed unheeded into its basin, now filled the garden with its rippling murmur. Quite close below her window a restless wagtail began to pipe his reedy song: "Sweet-pretty-creature"; and when he paused she could hear the young owls hissing from their nest in the ivy.

Mary gave up thoughts of sleep; there was only one sound she wanted to hear. Yet when it sent its muffled drumming across the fields, she drew in her breath sharply as she lay taut and concentrated. The hoof-beats of galloping horses! . . .

Who were the horsemen? Were they couriers from London,
sent to report the passing of new laws against Catholics? Were
they pursuivants, breathing hot on the trail of a hunted priest?
Would they draw rein only to spring from their horses and
bang on the door with their pikes? . . . Or would it be the
Harewell priest riding home to be in time for Mass in the morning? Mary was now at the window, but the road was on the
other side of the house. The hoof-beats grew louder, and she
could hear the commotion in the stable yard as the grooms
tried to quiet the barking dogs. The riders drew rein at the
stables; there was a confused murmur of voices. And how welcome was Mrs. Ardington's voice as she opened the door of
Mary's room to say softly: "We shall have Mass in the morning. . . . It is nearly midnight. Go to sleep, dear."

During her thanksgiving after her First Holy Communion
next morning, Mary offered her life to God, asking Him to
sanctify her that she might lead others to His love. When she
lifted her head she could see the priest making his thanksgiving,
his head bent in prayer; he had kept faith with the congregation. Mary's heart went out to him in gratitude. All her life she
was to experience that same reverence for priests; throughout
the years of her girlhood in Yorkshire they came into her life
bearing an aura of heroism which called out the generosity of
her own brave spirit. Before the sky in the east had reddened to
sunrise that September morning, the men and women who
had ridden to Mass remounted their horses and rode off into
the peaceful autumn countryside.

When barely fourteen Mary was again sought in marriage,
by Ralph Eldrington, another Northumbrian, "the person and
the estate," says Winefrid Wigmore "being competently ad-

vantageous." The *Painted Life* in the eighth of the series tells us of poor Eldrington's proposal. He looks a personable enough young man, and he has our sympathy for having to mention his offer of marriage, knowing well that a group of romantically-minded friends are watching at a distance. Mary says she will think it over, and we hear no more of Ralph Eldrington; for, even before the proposal, Mary had written her father a long, affectionate letter which Mrs. Ardington sent by special courier. Mary must have packed her grief into that letter, for Marmaduke Ward came at once to his tenderly-loved daughter. In the centre panel of the picture, we see her pleading with him, her little face looking drawn from fretting. The last panel tells us that her father is taking her home, and how happy she looks! The family have returned from the North to Newby Hall, and it is to that home, gay with the laughter and games of the younger brothers and sisters, that Mary turns her happy face. . . . She was then fourteen years old.

Her own comment on these proposals is fascinating. "Nor," she says, "after twelve years old did I ever see any that I did, or, for ought I know, could affect . . . it was ordinary with me to hate the party or parties in such extremity (especially when the marriage was offered to myself) as could not stand with Christian charity, and this towards several and for divers years together."

Winefrid thus continues the story of young Eldrington's rejection: "her dear and noble-hearted father, who had the greatest tenderness imaginable for her, broke it off, esteeming it as an aversion she had from that particular person, and that it would not be hard to find her her choice." Mary's own attitude aided this misunderstanding, for she says of herself: "I refused not those they offered forth of any desire to be religious, nor other reason, but because I could not affect them."

And then, looking back nineteen years, she cries to God, "But O Parent of parents and Friend of all friends, Thy intent in thus disposing was different. . . . What was there in me wherewith to serve Thee? Much less could I ever deserve to be chosen by Thee. O happy begun freedom, the beginning of all my good."

6. Babthorpe

"Sa beauté portait l'empreinte de la main divine qui l'avait pétrie "[1]

(CHATEAUBRIAND)

THE SPRING days at Newby Hall in the year 1600 were shadowed by the repeated rumours that Lord Huntingdon had spies watching everyone who came to or left Marmaduke Ward's household. Among Marmaduke's friends it was agreed that Huntingdon was bent on ruining him by fines, and, if need be, trumping up some excuse for clapping him into York prison. Messages from the Wards' friends in Northumbria begged them to return to the shelter of the Percys at Alnwick Castle. So once again Mary's parents packed their personal belongings, gathered their little family together, and set off for Northumbria. And again Mary was separated from that loved and loving home circle; for it was felt that the rigours of the northern climate would be too severe for her. Barbara clung to her in anguish as the good-byes were said. She felt that life was going to be intolerable without her cheerful elder sister, who, though she feared nothing, was always so understanding if one were frightened.

This time Mary was to be left at the home of Sir Ralph and Lady Babthorpe, close relatives of her mother. She had often visited Babthorpe Hall with her parents and had been slightly in awe of the number of fine lords and ladies who seemed to be

[1] "Her beauty bore the impress of the Divine Hand that had moulded it."

3 1

perfectly at home. As a matter of fact they probably were at home, for in that mansion, besides Sir Ralph and Lady Babthorpe, there lived two other knights with their wives; they were William Babthorpe and his wife (William was Sir Ralph's son) and Sir George Palmes and his wife (his lady was Sir Ralph's daughter). Besides these adults, there were six other children of Sir Ralph; a formidable household for a shy girl like Mary to have to meet. She felt forlorn enough after saying good-bye to her mother and little brothers and sisters at Newby Hall, and not even the ride with her father through the countryside lovely in the spring sunshine could make her view cheerfully the approaching exile from her home circle.

For an hour or so before they came within sight of the Babthorpe mansion they rode through the rich valley lands between the Ouse and the Derwent. Cows at pasture hardly bothered to look at the riders, for travellers passed up or down all day, and the fresh young grass was sweet. Carpets of bluebells under the trees by the roadside gave Mary the thrill of delight that was always her response to their beauty. Her father was glad to see her spirits lifting from their sadness, and as the horses were tired and the end of the journey almost in sight they ambled quietly along the edge of the road where the grass made quiet going. Tits fluttered and chirped among the clumps of hazels, and occasionally a black-necked pheasant would rise as they approached, to wing its way across the meadow, its plumage glinting in the sunlight. At last as they came to the crest of a hillock, the riders could see the spires of the village church and turrets pressed against the skyline. "Look!" said her father, "Babthorpe!"

Set in spacious parks, the ancestral home of the Babthorpes had adapted itself over the years to the architecture of the

periods. The old medieval gate-house had given place to beautiful wrought-iron gates which opened on to a sweep of
gravelled drive leading to the front porch where Ionic columns
showed that the architect had given scope to his admiration
for the classical orders. Parapets and balustrades showed further engraftings on the original pre-Renaissance mansion, and
gave a very pleasing appearance to the home that was to be
Mary's for nearly seven years.

When they sat down to meals in the large dining-hall, with
its oak panelling meeting the rich tapestries on every wall,
Mary could see on the coloured-glass windows the armorial
bearings of all the noble families with whom the Babthorpes
were related. And the fifteen-year-old girl, one fancies, would
have been less than human if she had not been delighted to see
among them the coat-of-arms of the Ward family. In Mary's
case, any temptations to pride became her first steps to heroic
humility. Fastidious and beautiful in appearance, she forced
herself one night to sleep with a kitchen-maid who was suffering from a skin complaint. A few days later, when she saw in
her mirror the spotty rash on her face, she shuddered, but
went about as usual until Lady Babthorpe, discovering what
had happened, gave her remedies—and a scolding.

Before summer had enveloped the countryside in its ripening
warmth, Mary had settled in to the life at Babthorpe. The eldest
brother, William, had returned some time before from the
Jesuit College at St. Omer where two younger brothers were
beginning their course, soon to be joined by Mary's brother
John. The Babthorpes were a happy family. Barbara, eight
years old, needed no bidding from her mother that she was to
make Mary feel at home—she became almost her shadow. And,
with the name of Barbara, the little girl slipped into Mary's

heart as a sister. Lessons in Italian and Latin were part of the
day's study programme, although Mary was already well
versed in both. But it was a gay household; guests seemed to be
always coming or going, and Mary had to meet them all, for
Lady Babthorpe treated her as her own daughter. To Mary's
delight she asked her to take the care of the chapel as her special duty, helped by an elderly servant, Margaret Garett.
While they were polishing brasses or mending altar-linen, a
friendship grew between them, and many years later Mary
noted in her autobiography that one of the many graces that
came to her at Babthorpe was this friendship with Margaret
Garett, of whom she wrote: "I trust in Jesus that she hath a
great crown in Heaven for the good my soul gained by her
means."

One day when they were sitting sewing in the linen room
upstairs (her cousin Barbara being present, of course) Margaret Garett was going over, for the entertainment of the girls,
incidents that had happened in her girlhood. When she talked
of a convent where she used to visit, Mary became very attentive. Margaret answered her questions to the best of her
ability and memory: "They were very holy women, Miss
Mary, and their beautiful lives of adoration gave great glory
to God. Ah, but it was a cruel thing to drive them from their
convents. There are no nuns in England at all now, and I hope
I shall never see those holy houses as they say they are today."
Then the old servant told the girls about a nun who had accepted some present without the Superior's permission. She had
to do penance for this fault against her vow of poverty. Margaret was a bit vague about the details, but Mary was deeply
impressed by the thought of the holiness of life required in a
nun, and she noted many years later: "It was then for the first

time that I found myself moved to love a religious life . . . and God gave me at that instant such a desire never to love any but Him that I have never wavered from that day in my purpose of belonging wholly to Him. . . ."

With this came the realization of what she had been about when, still almost a child, she had pushed away her suitors: "If one man," she says, "should or could be indued with the excellencies of all men together, yet were it impossible for me to content myself with the election of so little a good."

She knew little of the varieties of the religious life, and we can see perhaps the urge of the very special vocation that was to be hers in the comment she makes at this stage: "I had no inclination to any Order in particular, only I was resolved within myself to take the most strict and secluded, thinking and often saying, that as women did not know how to do good except to themselves (a penuriousness which I resented enough even then) I would do in earnest what I did."

Mary kept her secret to herself. She felt sure that God had called her in a special way to live for Him, though, as there were no convents left in England, she saw no way as yet of following up her vocation.

Towards the end of the summer the family went to their property at Osgodby, and Lady Babthorpe shared with them many of the precious memories the place held for her. In the early days of her married life when her father-in-law, Sir William Babthorpe, lived there, she had made her confession to the Jesuit martyr, Edmund Campion, who was Sir William's guest for a week or so. That was in February, 1581. One Sunday when all the neighbours had come in for Mass he gave them a sermon on the Ten Lepers. "When he spoke of Our Lord," she said, "he seemed to lead you into the Divine Presence. . . . He left us suddenly. He could stay nowhere long. Everyone was speaking about him, and there was a special search afoot for his capture. They caught him the following July."

Back in Babthorpe Hall Mary felt renewed interest in her martyred countrymen, many of whom were relatives or connections of the Wards. The Babthorpe chaplain, Father Mush, was writing the biography of Margaret Clitheroe, whose confessor he had been—she had met death for sheltering him in her home. Over in the Ingleby home at Ripley Castle there were hallowed memories of Mary's cousin, Francis, whom Margaret had also sheltered, and who in his turn met his martyrdom through torture. By the middle of 1601 the glorious roll of honour of Yorkshire priests bore two more names from among Mary's relatives. They were Edward Thwing and Robert Middelton, who gave up their lives for the faith in Lancaster. Years later in her autobiography Mary was to write: "I had during these years burning desires to be a martyr, and my mind was for a long time fixed upon that happy course; the sufferings of the martyrs seemed to me delightful for attaining to so great a good, and my favourite thoughts were, How? and When?" Only gradually did the Holy Spirit teach her that it was a spiritual rather than a bodily martyrdom that was to be her destiny. "Through certain occurrences," she says, "it pleased God for the present to moderate the vehemence of these aspirations, in order, as I believe, that I might take breath and apply myself to follow my vocation to the religious life."

She tried to withdraw from the social life of Babthorpe. But on this point her hostess was almost stern. She insisted on Mary's dressing suitably and sharing the life of the house.

Mary became ingenious in finding ways of mortifying her pride and what she called her self-esteem. She would ask a maid to give her overalls and a little job of work to do, the idea being chiefly that passing guests should think her one of the maids. . . . One morning there was a gathering of guests bent on a hawking expedition, several of them as yet unknown to her. As it was still early morning and the maids were at work, no one noticed a maid with a cloth and a pail of water washing the red-tiled lobby. If they had noticed her, they would have thought there must be better ways of washing a floor. Some of the young gentlemen jumped over the wet floor—it seemed to stay wet far too long. But the lads were kind and made no remark; still less did they glance at the hot-faced little maid. When they saw her that evening dressed in her rose brocade and cream ruff they were all attention to Mistress Mary Ward, the lovely daughter of Marmaduke. And Mary smiled.

The young nobility of Yorkshire who came and went, enjoying what seemed open hospitality at Babthorpe Hall, belonged to the landed gentry of that county. Cut off from the national life by their religion, they stayed at home, cultivating their estates, or escaped across the Channel to pursue their fortunes in freedom. Those who remained in Yorkshire, paying, like the Babthorpes, heavy recusancy fines, grew poorer each year in worldly goods, but they will have honour for all eternity for keeping alive the spark of the faith in England during those tragic penal years. They formed what we would now call a Catholic underground, or a resistance movement, building their hopes on the fact that the next ruler of England would most likely be the son of Mary, Queen of Scots, to whom nearly all of them had been ardently devoted. They argued that her son, James Stuart, would be almost in honour bound to lighten their burden.

One day during the year 1602 there was quiet jubilation at Babthorpe, for Thomas Percy had arrived from Alnwick Castle in Northumberland with an important letter to show them. He had been sent by his cousin, the Earl, to the court of King James at Edinburgh to ask his purpose towards Catholics in the event of his becoming King of England after Elizabeth's death, which could now be a matter only of months. In a letter to Thomas Percy, James had written the reassuring sentence: "As for the Catholics I will neither persecute any that will be quiet and give but an outward obedience to the law; neither will I spare to advance any of them that will by good service worthily deserve it." Here, indeed, was hope! The young men spoke of what they would do when they went to the university; and of what it must feel like to be a free man in your own country. They felt there was nothing they would not do for James Stuart when he became their king, if only he would allow them to keep their Catholic faith.

Sir Ralph and his wife, who had already suffered much in prison and by fines for their faith, were guarded in their optimism, although they were glad to see the hopeful enthusiasm of the young people. Mary thought it all over, and prayed that all would be well. Her thought flew to the home circle now sheltering at Alnwick Castle. It was rather concerning them than King James that she had plied Uncle Thomas Percy with questions; the letters he had brought her from them seemed to her as important as the letter of state which had put them all into such excitement. Still, she was genuinely glad to see all the young men so sanguine of the future.

One of the pleasures enjoyed in the autumn and winter

evenings was to gather for music in the large oak parlour where a fire burned on the hearth and the curtains were drawn. . . . One evening, Sir George returned after a visit to London bringing a young friend, a Yorkshire knight who had fallen under the spell of Shakespeare's plays, then being performed in the newly built Globe Theatre. . . . Both young men had been to see *Twelfth Night* several times; it seemed to be the hit of the year in London. Nearly all the young men could play the lute, even if their singing voices were only passable. Sir Ralph asked if they had heard anything of Master William Byrd while in London. "Oh yes," said Sir George, "Byrd still has power to soothe the Queen with his music. She dotes on his madrigals, pretending not to remember that he is a practising Catholic. And there he is, in the Queen's favour, yet paying his recusancy fines every month." . . . After the music they all went to the chapel for night prayers; everyone in the house would be at Mass in the morning.

At any hour of the day, if you went to the chapel, you would find someone there in prayer. Nearly everyone made a meditation of an hour or a half-hour, and in the afternoon at four o'clock they had Evensong and Matins. We know this on the word of Father Pollard, a Jesuit who was the chaplain for different periods while Mary was at Babthorpe. It was there that she first met the Jesuits who were to become her lifelong friends, chief of whom were Father John Gerard and Father Holtby, who was Mary's spiritual director for the seven years of her stay at Babthorpe. Months, sometimes a year, would pass without an opportunity of speaking with him, for like all the other priests on the English Mission, the Jesuits were continually travelling in the service of their flock. Since the arrival of the first two Jesuits, Parsons and Edmund Campion, in 1580, there had been a steady stream, so that by the turn of the century there were forty-five of them, expecting every day to meet torture and martyrdom. They were particularly hated by the Elizabethan government, as their closely knit organization made them a more formidable body than the secular priests, who, without bishops to guide them, were more easily thwarted in their missions, in spite of their great personal holiness and bravery. One of the sad things that will be told in this book is the growth of misunderstandings, amounting often to intense rancour, that grew up in England between the Jesuits and the secular clergy, just at a time when their union would have been such a support to the Catholics. The destiny of Mary Ward, humanly speaking so tragic, was to have her life beaten out on this anvil. But for the present all that suffering was mercifully hidden from her. The one suffering that she now saw clearly was the plight of the Yorkshire Catholics and her inability to do anything to save the faith in her country. It was quite clear to everyone that the object of the Penal Laws was to outlaw and ruin the whole of the Catholic community.

On the night of the 26th of March, 1603, as they left the chapel after night prayers, a galloping horseman turned in the park gates and drew rein at the front porch. He was Sir Ralph's private courier from London, bringing the news that Queen Elizabeth was dead. For weeks they had been hearing reports of the old queen's mental distress in the face of death, of how she had confided to Lady Scrope that she had seen a hideous vision of her own body, "exceeding lean and fearful in a light of fire." Conscience had wakened to torment her. Thinking of these things, Mary slipped into the chapel again to pray for the soul of the dead queen, whose grandeur had been built up on so much human anguish. . . . Others in the party, who had assembled round the courier on the porch, asked questions about James. Yes, Sir Roland Carey himself had ridden to Scotland to inform him that he was King of England. The young men at Babthorpe that night could hardly restrain their excitement. Surely, in God's name, a new chapter was beginning.

In a few days, on a crisp April morning when the cuckoos were sending their clear notes from every corner of the garden, James Stuart with his retinue rode down the highway from Edinburgh into the city of York on his way to London, where he was to be crowned King of England, with the title of James I. While he paused for a few hours in York for a rest and a change of horses, spokesmen from among the Catholic gentry of the county waited on him, testifying their loyalty to the crown which he would wear and welcoming him with sincere hearts to England. Among these gentlemen was Father John Gerard's brother, Thomas Gerard, to whom King James expressed gratitude for the loyalty of the Gerard family to the King's mother. Said James: "I am particularly bound to love your blood on account of the persecution you have borne for me." That evening at Babthorpe Hall, ten miles out of York, Thomas told a houseful of friends of the good omen of his encounter with King James. He did not say how repulsive he found him, with his gluttonous, undignified manners and his general air of unkingliness.

Lying, perfidious James! Hardly was his coronation over when he embarked on a course of persecution against Catholics. Early in 1604 he issued a proclamation ordering all priests to leave England within a month, and all the Elizabethan laws with their penalties were re-enacted. Robert Cecil, who had been made Secretary of State in 1596, continued to be what he had now been for many years, the virtual ruler of England. Once James had shown what a great fellow he was against the Catholics, he felt Cecil would be his loyal servant.

7. Farewell to England

*"Tu lascerai ogni cosa diletta più cara-
mente."*[1]

(DANTE)

THE PERFIDY of King James I is now matter for history, but
to the English Catholics of that era it came as something so
diabolical that they could hardly believe their senses. The
Yorkshire gentlemen who had received his promises were
stunned by his dastardly proclamation of 1604. Honest, fearless and forthright themselves, they could not imagine why any
man should so meanly lie to a fellow-man, as James had lied
to them. But there was worse to come: "It seems impossible,"
says E. I. Watkin, "to discover the true story of the Gunpowder Plot. . . . The body of English Catholics had no part in
it, no knowledge of it, no approval of it. Commemorated, however, by a service in the Prayer Book, it counted against them
for centuries and did good service to the anti-Catholic tradition."[2]

It is probable that some beginning of a plot became known
to Robert Cecil, perhaps through the renegade Lord Mont-
eagle's information; that he nursed it sedulously with the aid
of this same nobleman and "staged the dramatic discovery." It

---

[1] "Thou shalt leave every thing most dearly loved."
[2] *Roman Catholicism in England from the Reformation to 1950* (Home
University Library of Modern Knowledge, Oxford University Press, New
York and London, 1957).

would not be the first time that a Cecil had borne such a part
—"plots" under Elizabeth not uncommonly originated from
that highly talented family: it has been in fact suggested that
this was one of them.[3] Anyhow, whether Robert Cecil started
it or only fomented it, the Plot gave a wonderful excuse for
further anti-Catholic legislation, especially against the laity.
Communion must now be received yearly in the parish church,
householders were made responsible for the recusancy of guest
or servant, Catholics must not reside within ten miles of
London or practise as lawyers, doctors, judges, clerks, stew-
ards, officers of courts or corporations; serve as officers in army
or navy. Old penalties were strengthened or renewed: they
might not journey more than five miles from home, and rec-
onciling a convert or being reconciled became treason abroad
as well as at home.

Of course the household at Babthorpe guessed nothing of
what was afoot. Mary's uncles, the Wright brothers and
Thomas Percy, and her cousins the Winters seemed too busy
and tense to take part in any social life, and rarely visited Babthorpe that year; and her own personal problems were in the
forefront of Mary's mind. She steeled herself to accept the fact
that if she was to serve God in the way that her conscience demanded (and all the graces received in prayer left her in no
doubt on that point), she would have to say good-bye to her
family and her country and to become a nun in some convent
across the Channel. Occasionally she heard of young English
gentlewomen doing this. So, why not she? But beyond speaking on the subject to Father Holtby in confession and receiving
encouragement from him, Mary took no one into her confidence.

3 See Hugh Ross Williamson, *The Gunpowder Plot*.

The Babthorpe household who saw her every day would have been dull-witted indeed not to see that she had her face turned towards an ideal about which they felt little doubt. They had only to see her interest when any visitor who had been out of England spoke of convents in Flanders where nuns lived in silence and charity, giving great glory to God and praying for their persecuted co-religionists in England. Towards the end of 1604 the whole household knew that Mary intended going overseas to become a nun, but she found not one in the house to support her plan. Everyone, from Sir Ralph and his wife down to the gardeners and kitchen-maids, showed their love for her by pleading against her religious vocation. How could they live without her? Didn't she realize how much good she was doing by her mere presence among them? Surely she knew that her health would never hold out in the rigours of convent life? "The danger," she says, "that I might be forced to return to the world through the failure of my bodily powers, was the only thing among all they said which made any impression on me."

A gentleman who caught sight of her face one day as she came from the chapel marvelled at its serene beauty; she seemed to radiate peace, and for a troubled moment he dreaded lest he should be the disturber of that peace.

This man was Edmund Neville, heir to the Earldom of Westmoreland, and he had made up his mind to ask Mary to marry him. Unknown to Mary, her father had encouraged him in his suit and had written to Sir Ralph and Lady Babthorpe on the matter. To all the planners it seemed the ideal marriage, for Neville, although twice Mary's age, was a fine character and a loyal Catholic; and Sir Ralph and his wife had reported to Marmaduke that Mary liked and admired him. As she walked along the gallery she turned her head towards the window in an alcove where Neville was standing, and her face lighted up with a smile as she went towards him. . . .

By the time they had walked to the end of the gallery and paused at the open window to admire the rose-garden, he had summoned up his courage. . . . Very gently Mary refused the honour, confiding in him her aspirations to the religious life. Neville said that he too had felt that way some years before, and that he had even spent some months at the English seminary in Rheims; but that when it appeared that he would succeed to the earldom a holy priest had advised him to return to England and find a Catholic wife who would help him to keep the faith for the counties of the north.

Westmoreland, as we know, was an important earldom, and its importance was recognized by Shakespeare, who put several of its successive earls into his historical plays, following closely the chronicles of Holinshed. If Edmund Neville did not contest the title it would go to a heretic.

And now he smiled ruefully as he said to Mary: "I will never contest it without you at my side." Then he told her that her father favoured the alliance and was writing to her.

When it became known that Mary had refused her suitor, she felt that everyone at Babthorpe was out of sympathy with her—as indeed they were (all except little Barbara, who was sure Mary was right whatever she did). So deeply was Mary suffering over the new complication in her affairs that she could not discuss it with anyone. Her confessor, Father Holtby, was in London, and she did not easily open her heart in confession or anywhere else. So she nerved herself to face her father, who had written a second letter on receiving news of

Neville's rejection. The tone of his letter was such that she could expect only a very unpleasant and painful interview. But as often happens in such a crisis she received such interior enlightenment and fortitude from the Holy Spirit that she was quite ready to go overseas at once—so sure was she that a religious vocation was God's design for her. All her doubts had fled never to return on that subject.

Then her father arrived. She had a bad moment as she kissed him: he looked so thin and worn, his hair grey at the temples. After the messages from her mother and John and Barbara and Elizabeth, and even from little Teresa and George, he came straight to the point of his visit: Was it true she had rejected Edmund Neville's offer of marriage? Did she realize that as Countess of Westmoreland she could make her home a rallying point for all the persecuted Catholics of the North?— and God knew there were enough of them falling away. Did she care so little for the sufferings of her people that she could so lightly put aside what was clearly her duty?. . . . Mary went to the chapel, her pulses racing with the emotional strain, her knees shaking as she knelt. Then, peace.

When she saw her father next morning he had calmed down, but was looking haggard. Mary said quietly that she would go at once to London if he would allow her, and that someone would get her a passage to Flanders. Her father guessed, perhaps, that she had endured about as much as body and spirit could stand, so he said: "We shall go together, and we can see Father Holtby in London; he will see clearly what ought to be done." So on a lovely autumn day at the end of October 1605, father and daughter set out on their last ride together.

Because of the danger of attacks by highwaymen, they went their long journey in a large party, two maids for Mary, and a number of serving-men with the pack-horses, besides some friends of the Wards from Yorkshire, all the men armed with daggers and swords. But Mary and her father often rode for miles slightly apart from the others, enjoying the russet glory of the country sights and sounds so dear to both. In Derbyshire they could see to their right for miles as they rode the sweep of the moors, and occasionally they saw grouse or a covey of partridges.

By the fifth of November they were riding through Warwickshire, where the party broke up, Mary and some attendants going to other relatives, while her father rode on to the home of Thomas Percy and his wife. It was probably on this journey to London that Marmaduke Ward became unwittingly involved in the troubles of the Gunpowder Plot. The conspirators, having failed, were riding north—and most of them were relatives of the Wards: the brothers Wright, killed on November 8 in an encounter with the sheriff's officers, and Thomas Percy, mortally wounded and dying shortly afterwards in the Tower, were Mary's uncles; others of the conspirators and Ambrose Rookwood, executed for providing them with horses, were her cousins. Marmaduke Ward was arrested, brought before two magistrates and questioned about the escaping conspirators. He had not known, he said, "of the companies passing that way until they came to Alcester, nor of their purpose anything at all." But there he was in the midst of the confusion, in the very house of Thomas Percy's wife! Only his record of complete aloofness from politics saved him; and with thankful if sorrowful hearts father and daughter rejoined each other and set forth again towards London, hardly daring to discuss aloud the tragic happenings of those November days. The sight of the fine new mansions being built, often with stone from dismantled monasteries, proved what they had often heard: that a new wealthy class was growing up, many of whom were battening on the rewards of their apostasy from the Catholic faith. Yorkshire had fewer of these than the counties near London. But, *How long, O Lord, how long?* must have been the agonized prayer of many a Catholic.

Finally, just a fortnight after leaving York, the party rode into London, Mary and her father going to the London house of some friends at Baldwin's Gardens, a suburb of stately homes. Here Marmaduke had arranged to meet Father Holtby, whose kind welcome could not conceal his deep anxiety over the fate of his Superior, Father Garnett; for it was now commonly known that Robert Catesby had told him in confession of his guilt in the Gunpowder Plot. Farther Garnett had done all he could to persuade him to give up the idea, but he could do no more than that, having received Catesby's confidence under the seal of confession. Although the priest was not captured until the following January, a relentless search was being made for him, to the great anxiety of all the Jesuits, of whom Father Holtby was now in temporary charge. A bitter search was also being made for Father John Gerard, who was a close friend of most of the conspirators. So, as Mary, her father and Father Holtby chatted and exchanged their greetings with their usual warm courtesy, each had a private worry. We know well what Mary and her father were thinking about. Of the three, Mary probably felt the most cheerful, for Father Holtby's presence gave her, as she thought, a strong ally. Next morning before Mass, which was said in the house, the priest asked Mary to confer with him. Although she knew he had been speaking with her father—and surmised the subject—she was quite unprepared for the heavy words he pronounced, for he said in effect that she should by no means leave England, nor become a religious, and that her duty was to marry Edmund Neville.

Writing later, Mary recorded that these words "caused me inexpressible distress, because I did not dare to do what he prohibited as unlawful, nor could I embrace that which he proposed as my greater good." An early biographer to whom she told the incident tells us that, going into the chapel, "she cast herself at the feet of her dear Lord Jesus Christ, her good Master, and said 'it was He must answer for her,' and then, in holy quiet, free from noise and motion of any exterior things, rested in herself, united with God in a profound peace and tranquillity, remaining interiorly recollected and motionless, and as if insensible." Meanwhile the priest came in and Mass began. After Mass Mary went to the adjoining alcove where the priest was washing his hands, and, as she had always done as sacristan at Babthorpe, offered him the hand-towel. She saw that tears were running down his face as he murmured brokenly: "What, is it then possible, shall I live to offend my God?" Then, turning to the girl, he said: "I will never more hinder your religious design and holy resolution, but further you all I can. . . ." An accident at Mass had caused him to spill the precious contents of the consecrated chalice, and with his distress came a heavenly light on God's will for Mary Ward. Father Holtby spoke to Marmaduke, who, accepting the change of heart, talked no more of Edmund Neville, but joined with Father Holtby in preparing letters for priests and friends in St. Omer, where the English Jesuits had a college for the education of the sons of the Catholic gentry of England —at least for those who could evade the government spies; for it was a punishable offence for parents to send their children abroad to be educated.

It seemed there would be no passage for Mary until well into the new year of 1606, so her father left her with a chaperone, accustomed to caring for Catholic girls escaping from England. Our artist of the *Painted Life*, making a double panel of the farewell and the sailing, shows us father and daughter, father advising her to be prudent and to be sure to let him know if she was unhappy and wanted to come home. (The affectionate father is the same in every century as he says good-bye with breaking heart to the daughter called from the home nest to heavenly flights of grace.) One last word, a quick embrace, and the parting is over for Mary and her father. As for Edmund Neville, he became a Jesuit in Rome, and returned to England, where he died at the age of eighty-five, "a noble confessor of Christ," after an illness resulting from nine months of chains, cold and hunger in a foul prison.

A favourable opportunity for the crossing to St. Omer did not occur until May, as it was becoming increasingly dangerous for any sea-captain to take a Catholic passenger without a license to travel. Knowing well it would be refused, the Wards had not applied for one for Mary. So for her it was flight, after the captain had been handsomely paid for his risk.

"Setting forth," says Mary, "upon the so greatly desired journey, and not yet out of England, a great obscurity darkened my mind and doubts rose up within me, as to where and in what religious order I should have to remain, and in this darkness and disquiet of soul I passed the sea and arrived at St. Omer."

The artist, who gives us the picture of the embarkation, has several things which he feels he must tell us. He expects us to understand that the boat was not quite so small, nor quite so crowded, nor quite so full of sail. But he has to tell us that fair stood the wind for Flanders; that the captain, hat in hand, considered his wealthy passenger a great catch, and that the day was so fine that Mary did not even have to wear a coat. . . . They did indeed have a good crossing, and by the time Mary set foot on the soil of Flanders her resolute will had overcome her fears, and she felt her heart lifting as she heard the chiming of church bells calling the people to Mass. This was something she had never heard before.

8. Obscure Ways

*"Shown, O Lord, Thy ways to me; and teach
me Thy paths."*

(PS. 24)

IT WAS characteristic of Mary's singleness of purpose that on arriving at St. Omer she went straight to the Jesuit College with her letters. She would have been welcome at many homes of English exiles, family friends; but, having broken her earthly ties of tenderness, she made no attempt to seek solace by forming new ones. One contact she could have permitted herself, we might argue, was with her cousin, Lady Mary Percy, who in 1598 had founded in Brussels a Benedictine convent for Englishwomen. If Mary's thoughts strayed in that direction, she headed them off as she walked up the street to present Father Holtby's letter at the Jesuit College. (Did she even ask to see the Babthorpe boys? We think not.)

As she waited for the Rector, a priest, Father George Keynes, looked into the room. When he found out why she was there, his face lit up: Of course, she was just the person the Poor Clares were waiting for. How providential! Mary was hearing of them for the first time in connection with her vocation. So they were waiting for her? How strange! By the time the Rector appeared, the whole matter had been settled greatly to the satisfaction of Father Keynes (whose name receives a more or less sharp thrust in every biography of Mary Ward). He took the Rector aside before Mary could speak for herself, and unfolded his providential plan. He was evidently very convincing, for when Mary began a murmured remonstrance, the Rector glanced at her to say: "Nay, gentlewoman. . . ." What a phrase for some author's Lost Diaries.[1] What came after? We shall never know, for Mary broke off there in her journal.

Within a few hours, with a letter from Father Keynes, she was waiting in the dim little parlour of the convent of the Poor Clares, trying to think clearly about the situation into which she had been manoeuvred. The priest had said these nuns were in great need of an out-door sister—a lay-sister, of course. But she would not mind that, would she? No, she would willingly be a lay-sister. But out-door? The priest had brushed that aside, assuring her that she would not always be out, that she would be able to devote just as much time to meditation as the choir sisters, that this was God's will for her. "I remained silent," she says, "feeling an extreme repugnance to accept their offers. But arguing interiorly with myself, it appeared to me that, the rules being the same, and the place proposed to me only more abject and contemptible, the repugnance and aversion which I felt could spring from nothing but pride."

Next morning early, in a plain dress, with a big basket on her arm, she was out on the street to beg food for the community. When she returned to the convent at midday the basket was full; again, in the evening. So day after day she went out, and the good people of St. Omer gave her food because of her sweet, tired face and her graceful, regal bearing that no lumpish garments could hide. After a month she was received as a lay-sister novice; the begging continued, but now with another sister, as custom demanded. Though still young, Mary had

[1] Cf. *Lost Diaries* by Maurice Baring.

gone with swift steps along the way of holiness since she had with such docility obeyed the voice of Father Keynes directing her to be an out-door sister with the Poor Clares. Later, she said that her repugnance to his direction was so strong that to obey was like stepping into boiling oil. Once she broke down physically, but got up from her bed and went on begging, "despite an impostume on her knee" which had to be poulticed for many months. The mental distress continued. "Turning myself therefore to God," she writes, "I applied myself to prayer with extreme diligence, entreating that the Divine will might be done . . . without regard to my content or consolation. . . . I declared, both to my confessor and to the Superiors of the monastery, the internal suffering which I felt and the exceeding difficulty which I found in embracing that vocation."

It is a strange story, and though Mary never seems to have felt any resentment she did come to realize that both Father Keynes and the Abbess had shown "little correspondence with my great sincerity to them."

They had told her the Rule she would follow as lay-sister was the same, but she found it to be totally different, the Rule in fact of the Third Order of St. Francis. She had hardly any time for prayer and meditation: she was on the road all day.

A lay-sister had, it seems, been badly wanted, and the needs of the convent had weighed more with them than Mary's own vocation. Father Keynes told her that should an angel from heaven tell her to depart, still she should stay, and Mary hearing in her mind the words: *he that heareth you, heareth Me,* accepted his orders "willingly, but with such an aversion and grief that death by any kind of torment I could imagine appeared most sweet." But what she would fain have escaped

"I now believe," she says, "to have been a thing which God willed, and a fitting way, at least seasonable, for what was to follow."

So when Father Keynes, seeing more of her worth, began to repent his action and himself became the angel urging her departure, Mary, relates Winefrid, answered "that by order she entered and by order would go out . . . before she entered she had no guide but her confessor, now the Superiors of the Order were hers, and were to dispose of her, accept or send her away as seemed best to them."

When she was out begging on hot days a fresh breeze would sometimes blow in from the English Channel. Then she would put down her heavy basket to wipe her forehead, thinking, as she often thought, of the sufferings "over there." As the Angelus rang out around her from convents and churches, she remembered those silent English Catholic bells and empty churches. Letters from home told of friends giving up their faith, unable to bear the intolerable burden of fines and recurring imprisonment in evil-smelling gaols. The Babthorpes were holding to their faith, but their sufferings were extreme. Not only was their property being filched from them, but Sir Ralph was now the target of a bitter campaign of hate. Each Sunday from the pulpits of Protestant churches he was calumniated. The very thought must have sickened Mary.

On the 12th of March, 1607, the feast of St. Gregory, as Mary and her companion came in at midday, they were told that the Father General of their order would be there for Visitation that afternoon, and that they need not go out again, as he would have to interview each member of the community privately. The information conveyed nothing to Mary, except that she would be able to spend some time in meditation in the chapel. It was St. Gregory's day; "my particular advocate," she calls him. She would spend the rest of the day praying for England, in which the great St. Gregory was surely still interested. He had sent the first missioners hundreds of years ago, he would again do something good for the English. . . . Moreover, "he would protect and help one of that nation." And Mary prayed to him "that I might live and die in the will of God and in the state which should most please His Divine Majesty." The Father General, a priest of great holiness and a keen observer, unexpectedly asked to speak to Mary, as the only Englishwoman there. She made no complaint even when he suggested that she should think well before going on to profession, but left herself completely in God's hands. There was a moment's silence. Then the priest said slowly: "My child, you are not for this state of life. Make your choice. I will serve you in whatever way I can."

Almost overwhelmed by such an unexpected turn of affairs, Mary returned to her sewing which she had put aside when called, a few minutes earlier—"returning to my work and devotions to St. Gregory" is her phrase. But it was to be a day of spiritual miracles for her; and she tells us: "I was on a sudden enkindled to procure a monastery for the English of this Order." She had been observant and womanly enough to see the great disadvantages that beset English ladies who entered this foreign order of nuns, where the food and customs made perseverance a rarity. Moreover, as French was the language used by all, they had to make their confessions in that language, and, apart from Latin books of devotion, to read in it also. Retiring to the chapel to pray about her inspiration, she "entreated Our Lord God that nothing I might do in this business should have other success than that which He willed . . .

and praying our most Blessed Lady and other saints to be wit-
nesses that my desires were no other but to do and have done
His Divine will."

In less than two months Mary was again in secular dress
(though a very quiet one)—an English lady of means in a
foreign country. Only a year had passed since her first arrival,
but her character had wonderfully matured in the hard school
of suffering. She seemed to have no bitter thoughts of anyone,
whether priest or nun, who had tried to direct her life; for she
was learning to realize the truth of the Portuguese proverb,
that God writes straight with crooked lines. She turned her
face to the work now in hand; the foundation of a convent
of Poor Clares for Englishwomen. The Father General was encouraging her, also the Bishop of St. Omer (Bishop Blaise),
who became her true friend. There was, moreover, much satisfaction at the Jesuit College, where the Fathers had for some
time seen the need but had been discouraged, as we see from
their report: "On our proposing the matter to our religious
friends and others, it was rejected by all as ridiculous."
All of these clerics must have been astonished, if amused
and pleased, when Mary announced that she had bought a large
house and was ready to begin at once. (Her dowry, returned
to her on leaving the convent, was in hand to pay expenses.)
"You realize, surely, good gentlewoman, that no religious
foundation can be made without permission of all the secular
authorities involved?" So Mary, with characteristic bravery,
decide to begin at the top, and went off to Brussels to interview the Archduke Charles and his wife, the Infanta Isabella,
the rulers of the Low Countries.
She went straight to see her cousin Lady Mary Percy at the

Benedictine convent, where the Infanta Isabella was a frequent
visitor. It was then an easy matter for Mary Ward to be granted
an audience at the royal court of Brussels. Among the tyran-
nical Spanish rulers who had from there dominated the countryside, tho Archduke Albert and Isabella stand out as a pleasant contrast. As regents for the King of Spain, the father of
Isabella, they kept their court in Brussels in the grand Spanish
manner celebrated in the pictures of El Greco and Velásquez.
The genuine piety of the Archdukes (as they were often
called) kept the grand manner from degenerating into a hard
worldliness. There were many Spanish grandees in their en-
tourage who looked with great interest at the beautiful English lady who was now often to be seen walking along the
heavily tapestried corridors to Isabella's private suite—for both
Albert and Isabella took an instant liking to Mary, an affection
that lasted all their lives.

In all, Mary was six months in and about the court at Brussels, feeling often desperate at the obstacles in the path of her
plans. To name two alone: she would have to sell the house
she had bought outside Gravelines, as no religious house was
allowed outside the town fortifications. Then, there was the
matter of confessors. She wanted English priests; and, as Jesuits were those she knew best, she wanted them. But it had
always been the custom that Poor Clare nuns should have Franciscan confessors, because of the identity of Rule and government. Finally, all these difficulties were settled, and the convent opened in Gravelines, with Father Roger Lee, S.J., as
confessor. Mary, though foundress, entered as a postulant with
a group of other English ladies who had been following the
preparations during the six months, and some of whom had
been in the other convent of Poor Clares. The novice-mistress

from there became the Superior, another opportunity of mortification for Mary, whose affectionate heart must often have felt chilled by the unfeeling government of this Superior. But having obtained the strictest Rule of Poor Clares, Mary embraced every hardship, settling into her new life in great peace.

The foundation prospered, and is still prospering in its numerous filiations. Some of these are in England, and surely in those houses everyone knows why, on the feast of St. Gregory every year, special prayers are said for the conversion of England. A house of Mary Ward's Poor Clares is in Sydney, Australia, doing good work. We make this digression to prepare our readers for what must now come: on May the 2nd, 1608, as Mary sat working with the other novices in great peace of mind, a sudden divine light showed her that she was not to be of the Order of St. Clare, but that God willed something else for her.

It was the first of these inexplicable intimations that Mary was to receive. "It appeared," she says, "wholly divine and came with such force that it annihilated me and reduced me to nothing. And there was no other operation in me but that which God caused; to see intellectually what was done and what was fulfilled in me, I willing or not willing, was all that remained to me." The experience would have been unbearable had not God supported her spirit and given her light to see that He had chosen for her another work, "greatly for His glory and for the utility of her neighbour and the good of others, particularly England." We can imagine the humiliations involved in the telling of her experience to her abbess and her confessor. The Abbess coldly said it was no longer the time when young ladies should have visions—penance, preferably the discipline, was what was needed. The confessor, Father

Roger Lee, was also inclined to severity, recommending her drily to a more exact observance of the Rule. Mary tried to obey both; in fact, did obey them, until she looked like death. Nor did she make any difficulty about a further trial of six or seven months. "I loved what I possessed," she writes, "most sensibly and before all things I knew . . . I wept to remember that I was not to be in that Order. And . . . I found myself already wearied out with the little labour taken in this foundation." She found not one soul to encourage her, but found "a special and fatherly assistance from God." Finally, when Father Lee saw that she was being led by ways he could not see, he gave what one, almost despairing, might consider a permission, saying: "You may be saved whether you go or stay." Not exactly a blessing.

After making over most of her property to the foundation, she bought a secular dress and went out again into the world, no longer a rich English lady but a poor exiled woman looking for lodgings. Most of her friends probably felt she was a failure; some might be fairly understanding, but nevertheless hoping she would not hang on to them. "So peculiar, you know, this instability. Twelve months a lay-sister, six months a court lady, and now this, just when everyone was saying, 'What a marvellous woman she is to found a convent for English ladies.' What will be the next bright idea?" Mary, with her sensitive nature and keen perceptions, surely knew what was being said. Any doubts she had would be dispelled by the cries of children when they saw her: "Look at the runaway nun! . . . I say, there's the visionary. . . . Yes, yes, the false prophetess." And a stone or two would be the childish reinforcement of the adult abuse they were repeating.

Now that she was out of the convent, Father Lee did not

desert her, she choosing to keep him still as her confessor. With his consent she made a vow to become a religious when she should find an order that would help her work for the salvation of her countrymen. If nothing else offered, she vowed to become a Carmelite; then, again with the permission of her confessor, she vowed to spend some months in England "to do all the little I could for God and the good of those there, so as not to be idle in the meantime, and the better prepared for whatsoever God should call me to."

9. Visit to England

"Yea, in the night, my Soul, my daughter,
Cry,—clinging Heaven by the hems;
And lo, Christ walking on the water
Not of Genesareth, but Thames!"
(FRANCIS THOMPSON)

MARY SET foot again on English soil soon after Easter in 1609. She had learnt that God had a plan for her "very much to God's honour, and the good of others, particularly England." Fortified also by the enlightened guidance of her director, Father Roger Lee, she was aware that the six months in England (he had set that limit for her) were to be a decisive experience; she was either to find some special work for souls or she was to return to St. Omer to become a Carmelite. Her vow of obedience to Father Lee, though in later years it had a restrictive effect, relieved her of much anxiety as to the conduct and outcome of this unusual enterprise. Before he entered the Society of Jesus, he had been an adventurous hunter of souls, in company with Father Gerard, in fashionable and worldly circles in London, and he knew all the dangers Mary would encounter. So with his blessing she had sailed for England. She must have visited her parents, whose loving, unquestioning welcome would be balm to her lacerated heart. She stayed a few days, accepting their attentions and comforts and restoring her spirit in their understanding love. Although not as wealthy as they had been, they provided amply

63

for her wants in the way of wardrobe and the hire of lodgings in the Strand, then the fashionable quarter of London. An aura of dedication seemed to surround her, and her parents saw her on her way solaced and proud that God had called their daughter to His service.

As Mary had no wish to involve any of her home circle in her dangerous enterprise, she would not allow her sisters to join her, though she failed to hold out completely against Barbara. Teresa she encouraged in her desire to become a Carmelite—as she did, not long after this, in Belgium. Elizabeth—we had better say it at once—belied the promise of an affectionate sister and lived to be one of Mary's many sorrows. John, married and living in Yorkshire, was there to meet her; and George was about to sail for St. Omer to be a pupil at the Jesuit College. But except for fleeting visits, Mary saw little of her home as her apostolate took shape. Church history states that it was she who inaugurated the now indispensable Lay Apostolate. Her name, and her many relatives among the aristocracy, ensured her a welcome at all the fashionable social gatherings, to which she often went accompanied by her girlhood friend, Winefrid Wigmore. Oh yes, and Miss Barbara Ward argued, evidently very convincingly, that she ought to be with Mary —at least, sometimes. But there were some circles from which Mary held her back. That Mary herself, so inexperienced in the looser styles of worldliness, should have walked among the libertines with such immunity and ease can only be explained by the divine sanction given to her way of living. She was absorbed by a zeal for souls that was the overflow of her generous love for God. A hairshirt under that costly dress reminded her always that she was dedicated to a suffering Lord and that she must have no other thought but to win souls for Him.

One woman converted by Mary "as famous for her birth as enormous for her crime" spoke of her "bewitching power," and she seems to have brought back many to the Church, turned others from "libertine lives," and helped yet others towards the religious life. "As far as I may judge," she herself briefly remarks, "I did not spend that time ill."

In the midst of her activities she managed to fit, by day or perhaps oftener by night, an amazing amount of prayer—an hour's daily meditation, the psalms of the Book of Hours, litanies, rosaries, spiritual reading. One morning after "a cold and unsatisfactory meditation" she resolved to help a girl wanting to enter religion with the gift of a dowry. This is interesting as showing that though her own dowry had been poured out on building the convent at St. Omer, her parents had been able to replenish her supplies generously.

As she thought this over and "adorned [her] head at the mirror" while "dressing according to the fashion of the country," Mary received another supernatural visitation, similar to the first "but more singular and . . . with greater impetuosity, if greater there could be. I was abstracted out of my whole being, and it was shown to me with clearness and inexpressible certainty that I was not to be of the Order of St. Teresa, but that some other thing was determined for me, without all comparison more to the glory of God than my entrance into that holy religion would be. I did not see what that assured good thing would be, but the glory to God which was to come through it, showed itself inexplicably and so abundantly as to fill my soul in such a way that I remained for a good space without feeling or hearing anything but the sound, 'Glory, Glory, Glory.'"

Mary was not always in London. Some relatives, Sir Edward and Lady Poyntz of Iron Acton in Gloucestershire, asked her to their home and Mary accepted, enticed by the hope of conferring with the wealthy and influential Sir Edward on the condition of the Catholics in that part of the country. The ride through the countryside starred with the blossoms of May refreshed her, body and soul.

Pushing on to Iron Acton, which had been a gift of William the Conqueror to the early ancestor of Sir Edward Poyntz, Mary's party turned aside to take the road to Tobington Park, a country mansion where Sir Edward, with his wife and family, was in residence. As it was late in the evening the children, even the eldest daughter, Mary, had gone to bed; so that it was not until the morning that they met their visitor, who rose early and was walking up and down a garden path in the warm spring sunshine with Sir Edward when a young girl threw open a casement above the terrace and saw them. She was a beautiful girl of sixteen, Mary Poyntz; and having watched that stately lady below for a few moments she exclaimed to her mother: "See, there she is, through whose instructions God will save me!" Mary Ward, not hearing the words, but the voice, looked up and made a smiling gesture of invitation. The girl ran out to join her; thus began a lifelong friendship.

Mary Ward stayed something less than a week with the Poyntz family, who made little outings for her, among them a trip to their town house, The Court, in Iron Acton. One of the points of interest there was the room where Sir Walter

Raleigh in 1580 had smoked a pipe of tobacco—the first smoke in England. A servant, alarmed at what he thought was an internal fire, was all for dashing a pail of water over the smoker. In the galleries were portraits of Sir Edward's ancestors, for with the coming of Holbein to England about sixty years before, an impetus had been given to portrait painting. Sir Edward Poyntz was a fearless Catholic, figuring in a round-up by the Privy Council as "one who keepeth in his house two Jesuit priests and is himself altogether Jesuited." When Mary told his daughter of her hopes for some new religious foundation, the sixteen-year-old begged to be allowed to join her. It says much for the faith of Sir Edward and his wife, and for the trust they had in Mary Ward, that they gave their daughter into her keeping. Mary Ward returned to London, where towards the end of the summer Mary Poyntz joined her.

There is in the convent of the Institute of the Blessed Virgin Mary at Augsburg a portrait that needs some explanation. One half of the face is of a beautiful young girl, the other half is little more than a skull with a bit of worm-eaten flesh. It is a portrait Mary Poyntz had painted of herself to present to a young nobleman who, finding that she would not marry him, asked that at least he might have her portrait. We may imagine his recoil when a parcel, on being opened, displayed this gruesome picture. He hastily returned it; it had done its work. His name was known to the early nuns of the Institute, but it has been lost, and we know only that he became a confessor of the faith.

Another visit paid in these months was to the Rookwood family at Coldham Hall in Suffolk. A memory that was still poignant was the execution of Ambrose Rookwood in the January before Mary left England in 1606. His wife was Mary's cousin (Elizabeth Tyrwhitt), and it is still stirring to read her noble words as she watched from a window on that cold morning her adored husband dragged to execution. He called out to her to pray for him; to which she answered: "I will; and be of good courage, and offer thyself wholly to God. I for my part do as freely restore thee to God as He gave thee unto me." It was chiefly for the sake of this courageous cousin that Mary made the trip to Coldham Hall. The seventeenth picture in the *Painted Life* tells us briefly an incident which shows that Mary was more than a kind friend while with the Rookwoods. The inscription on the painting runs: "Mary at Coldham Hall in England by the touch of her hands and by friendly conversation so changed a very wealthy matron, who was quite hardened in heresy (and of which conversion, learned and spiritual men after many strenuous labours and exhortations, had despaired), that she called out: 'I will be a Catholic, confess my sins, and do all which belongs to a perfect conversion'; which, with great fervour, she afterwards accomplished."

But of all the people in Coldham Hall, the one who will hold our interest most permanently was Susanna Rookwood, the sister of Ambrose. About twenty-six years of age, a character of great integrity and fervour; we are not surprised that she and Mary were drawn together as kindred spirits. Susanna begged Mary to take her with her to St. Omer. Leaving her to make her preparations, Mary returned to London, with injunctions from Susanna to get in touch with Jane Browne, a cousin of Elizabeth Rookwood; and therefore connected with Mary. A fifth girl, sent by Providence into Mary's orbit, was Catherine Smith, the staunch daughter of an old Catholic family. Her zeal was also enkindled by the very sight of Mary. All this group of girls were supremely her disciples. All had a religious vocation and a vocation to the Apostolate. The exact shape either vocation was to take was not yet clear, but Mary, they were sure, would be shown what it was to be. In neither of her two great blinding experiences had she learnt any details, and it is a little difficult to know at what point the decision was made that their work should begin with a school for girls at St. Omer. Her "great good" she knew was to be especially for her native country, and the future of Catholic children in England weighed heavily upon her. She had met even among her own kindred those who conformed outwardly, waiting for the better times that might never come. What would their children be? It was hard enough even for the most steadfast to get Mass said for their families and dependents, priests to absolve them, books for their instruction.

The pace at which pupils came from England as soon as the school opened in St. Omer seems to show that it had been promised at least to some parents before Mary left England.

Back in London, Mary had taken up the threads of her apostolate among the fashionable throng who throughout the summer found a good deal of pleasure in floating in barges on the clear water of the Thames. During the warm hours of twilight they would go for excursions, sometimes calling at some of the islands where pleasure-grounds invited with music until the early hours of morning, when they rowed back to the city in the moonlight. Mary was able to do a good deal of work on those trips, for no one would suspect that the beautiful girl, so richly dressed, chatting at the end of the boat with a cavalier, was steadying his wavering faith. A contemporary chronicle says in period style: "Divers were withdrawn from libertine lives, others put out of occasions, and many that desired to be religious, and had not the means, were holpen and disposed so as they attained the effects. She assisted so many towards their being religious, as herself did not so much as know the persons, when by occasion of seeing her they acknowledged the grace of being religious to have come by her means."

One evening as she entered a river barge with its silken hangings she wondered why the lady with her had been so pressing in inviting her to go. She was not a person whom Mary would, in the ordinary way, have cared to go about with. She was cold-shouldered by the society beauties who still had a care for their reputations; it was the young gallants who competed for her smiles. As the two ladies took their seats in the barge, Mary wondered how they would find anything to talk about. Fortunately there was a good deal of singing and lute-playing, leaving scope for only desultory conversation. A clear baritone was singing one of the madrigals of the day, but Mary, enjoying the cool grey beauty of the river, was not following the words. At the end of the first verse her companion glanced at her, saying, "You know it, of course?" Mary confessed that she did not know the air and was not listening to the words. "Oh listen. . . ." The singer had begun the second verse:

> "For she is fair without compare,
> And fresh as blossoms are.
> Her shining eyes light up the skies
> As doth the morning star."

Mary's companion gave a hard little laugh: "That's you," she said, "only you're a dark beauty. Still, no matter, it's you all the same." Then, before she knew how it had come about, she was telling Mary the story of her recklessly squandered young womanhood. She ended by saying, "I've watched you for a long time; and you must have bewitched me, for I could not stand this secret burden any longer. . . . Now that you know, I hope you won't jump into the river to get away from me." But the pressure of Mary's fingers on her wrist, and the affectionate look in the deep, dark eyes, said No, to that. By now they had reached the landing-stage, and the unhappy girl had put on her gaily smiling mask, saying the night was just beginning for her, and offering to say good-night to Mary. But Mary insisted on taking her to her own lodgings. That was the beginning of a remarkable conversion.

Mary paid for this soul by a humiliation that quickly followed. It probably got round among some of the gallants that Mary was friendly with their light-minded friend. Whatever their reasoning, one of them, evidently of the new wealthy nobility, hoping to ingratiate himself with Mary, sent his footmen with sweets and preserved fruits to her lodgings on the following evening. The old record tells us that "she fearing, and not unjustly, that a snare of the wicked enemy might be hidden underneath, bolted herself into her room and passed the whole night in prayer and penance." She had sent the sweets back with the footmen; but she did well to bolt herself in her room, as a Jacobean gallant might well read into the rebuff a display of coyness.

It was high time for her to leave. People in fashionable circles in the Strand were beginning to notice the group of attractive young ladies, of whom at least one or two were always with Mary, so she made preparations "to go over the water," as unobtrusively as she could.

Before we let her go there is one more incident that asks to be told. It concerns one of Mary's Protestant relatives, a Miss Gray who lived in London. Accurate reports had let Mary know that she would have no success with her if she approached her as a Catholic relative, so Mary's quick mind hit on the idea of joining her staff of servants as a personal maid. With such opportunities of chatting, Mary soon had the lady out of love with heresy and desirous of becoming a Catholic. Mary's old friend, Father Holtby, S.J., was her collaborator in this conversion, as in many others during this sojourn in London. It must have been a happiness to him to see the flowering of her personality, rooted so securely in God's love. If he carried as a wound in his heart an accident at Mass in Baldwin's Gardens in November 1605, Mary had it inscribed in hers and in her little private note-book among her special graces: "1st— the spilling of the Chalice. . . ." Nothing is lost in the divine economy; humiliation and joy are two sides to the same coin that admits us into the kingdom of God's love, even on earth. This must have been in Mary's mind as she knelt for his farewell blessing.

The approach of autumn in the city was announced in cool, soft tones of evening mists that hung in veils of blue transparency over the river. On sunny days the golden glory of the trees was mirrored in its quiet waters. As Mary looked out on the scene from her windows, one half of her mind was planning busily for the return to St. Omer. She felt, not without cause, that her movements were being watched by unfriendly eyes. We may be sure that when the footmen returned that summer evening to their master with the "elegant collation" (the phrase is the chronicler's) the lordly young blade was irked enough to say in the language of his time and class (not necessarily high Jacobean): "Who does she think she is, any-way?" At the mildest he would have named her "a subtle wench" who was worth watching. Yes, Mary was wise to move off. Gathering her five companions together, she slipped away with them, all under assumed names, into the mists that hung over the Channel.

For the sake of prudence, Barbara Ward did not sail in the same boat—some Londoners were a little too interested in the movements of the Wards. She joined Mary shortly in St. Omer; at the same time as the other Barbara came from the Benedic-tine convent in Brussels to join the group. Mary had been in correspondence for some time with Barbara Babthorpe, who was fretting over the refusal of the abbess to receive her as a novice because of her voice, which had grown husky after some throat infection. The abbess kindly explained to the dis-appointed postulant that she would not be happy as a Bene-dictine nun, because of the community duty of singing the Office. There was satisfaction all round when Barbara Bab-thorpe took her place by Mary Ward, making the seventh of her first companions.

10. The Beginnings of the Institute

BEFORE THEY left England Mary must have given her companions a fairly clear idea of the life to which she was taking them. They would wear a simple, dark dress and veil in the manner of widows and would live as if bound by the vows of poverty, chastity and obedience, though they would not be religious. There would be hours of prayer (vocal and mental) and very little material comfort in the house; but she hoped they would all enjoy the peace that was the portion of those who dedicated their lives to God. Their special work would be the education of the girls who would be sent to them. She could see no further than that, she added, as she looked at the group questioningly. The purpose and enthusiasm shining in their faces had need only of murmured words of assent. Already they had the names of a dozen or more girls whose parents were only waiting for the school to open so that they might send them across. The ready response of all the parents consulted left no room for any anxiety on the score of pupils.

No better location could have been chosen than St. Omer, where the whole attitude of the townspeople was one of sympathy towards the English Catholics. It was the town where accurate news from home could always be obtained, for the English Jesuit College was in constant touch with the Catholic families on the other side. Among its pupils were brothers of nearly all the girls who would be sent to Mary Ward's school; brothers also of Mary and her seven companions, whose parents at home had ties of close friendship with one or other of the Jesuits at the College. Mary's friend and director, Father Roger Lee, was also one of the College staff, and was asked by Bishop Blaise of St. Omer to be the confessor and director of the group which, under Mary Ward's leadership, went into residence in a large house in the Grosse Rue. Before long the towns-folk were calling them the English Ladies—a name that in many countries they have kept to this day.

Besides the boarders brought to them by nearly every boat that came from England, there were girls sent as boarders from all the centres in Belgium where English exiles were living with their families. A free day-school opened for the girls of St. Omer was a novelty. In Bordeaux in France there was a similar school founded by Madame Lestonac, whose nuns were enclosed. But in St. Omer the English Ladies went with their pupils to the cathedral to Mass every morning. Hitherto, throughout Europe, the education of girls at convents was restricted to those whose parents were able and willing to send them to live within the convents all during their school years —no term-holidays, not even at the end of the year. You returned home only when your education was finished. Mary's actual school programme was advanced for those days; besides womanly accomplishments, languages were stressed. (It was here that the linguist, Winefrid Wigmore, worked up a tradition that has lasted for centuries in the European houses of the English Ladies.)[1] As the number of pupils increased, so fortunately did the applications from young ladies anxious to join Mary and her companions. One of the earliest of these was Anne Gage, living in exile with her parents in Belgium.

Although Mary welcomed the recruits, they added to her anxieties. Already friends, religious and secular, were pointing to their anomalous position—they were neither in the world nor out of it. Why not seek stability at once by taking steps either to join some well-established order or to have the Rule of one such order adapted for their needs? So ran leading questions and advice. Mary listened but felt that the way of the English Ladies was along an unformed road, at present shrouded in darkness. To obtain light on their problem as well as to train the souls of her company in asceticism, Mary arranged from the outset that they should lead lives of mortification. Right well they did: "She and her companions took food but once a day, slept only upon straw beds, and undertook penances and mortifications besides." Father Lohner adds: "A continual self-renunciation, a humble knowledge and acknowledgment of their own faults; simple obedience and subjection of their own will and understanding; . . . interior recollection and love of silence . . . were to be seen there." Wonder not, then, at his comment that "the Holy Spirit of God entirely possessed the house as His own, and richly endowed it with heavenly love."

Early in 1611 Mary took two or three of her companions across to England, where property settlements in their regard and collection of boarders' fees made a personal visit necessary. As she would not expose her "company" to the dangers of living with friends, she bought at once a house in London to be a

[1] See Appendix II.

pied à terre, where two or three could be in residence. She had hardly returned to St. Omer when an epidemic of measles broke out among the boarders. It could be a fearsome sickness in those days, and Mary, taking more than her share in nursing the patients, herself fell ill, so ill that her life was despaired of. That they might lose her was something not to be thought of: she was everything to her community—spiritual mother, friend, adviser; the cause, under God, of their departure from their devoted parents. If Mary were taken, there was no one to fill her place among the foundations that could well be described as shaky. So three or four of them, putting on their cloaks and wrapping a few belongings into bundles, set out on a pilgrimage to a shrine of Our Lady thirty or forty miles away —beyond Brussels, beyond Louvain. Our Lady heard their petition; Mary Ward was immediately cured, and ready to join the tired pilgrims in prayers of thanksgiving on their return.

There was now a matter of even greater moment that Mary had to share with them; something so wonderful, so supernatural, that she found difficulty in explaining it. But the joy her spiritual daughters read on her face prepared them for what she told them. After the sudden recovery from her illness, she rose and dressed, and later in the afternoon was resting "in some extraordinary repose of mind," when she "heard distinctly, not by sound of voice, but intellectually understood, these words: *'Take the same of the Society.'* " The few words gave such comfort and strength to her soul, that, as she explained, "It was impossible for me to doubt but that they came from Him, Whose words are works." Mary kept to herself the ominous words which ended the heavenly communication: "Father General will never permit it. Go to him." The conviction that divine providence had so manifestly indicated their next step gave a new impetus along the way of holiness to the English Ladies. Their prayers and mortifications became the expression of their thanksgiving even when darkness closed in on their way once more. And darkness did close in; for Father Roger Lee, to whom Mary recounted her grace of enlightenment, told her to dismiss the matter from her thoughts. His own alarm at the thought of "Jesuitesses" must have been sharpened by the consternation of his rector and several of his brethren. In Bordeaux two Jesuits had encouraged Madame Lestonac to found a congregation using the Rule of St. Ignatius adapted for women. But these nuns were enclosed and were under the jurisdiction of the bishop of the diocese; so theirs was another story. Mary Ward had no intention of having her nuns enclosed or under the government of a bishop. The idea of nuns moving from their enclosure and having a Mother General was completely repugnant to Catholic thought in the seventeenth century. "My confessor resisted," she wrote later; "all the Society opposed."

To return to the opposition of Father Lee, we find in an old record that "He carefully considered all that Mary had hitherto done, and being suddenly enlightened by heavenly light he used all his efforts to maintain the Institute." But it was only gradually that he showed his change of opinion. He and several Jesuits who thought well of her tried to persuade her to adopt Rules already in use for congregations of women; but Mary, thinking of the conversion of England and of the conditions that were likely to prevail there for many years to come, remained firm in her refusal of existing Rules. We, who see nuns out on errands of mercy or taking their pupils on educational excursions, and who know that nearly every order has a

Mother General, find it hard to realize the fierce opposition that Mary Ward had to face. Hers was the lonely way of the pioneer.

One Jesuit, from the beginning, never doubted that Mary was on the right road. He was Father John Gerard, who, after escaping from England in 1606 and going to Rome, had returned to Flanders to open a Jesuit novitiate for the English at Louvain in 1609. In England he had been closely associated with the parents and brothers of several of the English Ladies, had been a close friend of Ambrose Rookwood, of the Babthorpes, the Wigmores, the Vauxs, and knew the Wards. The parents of most of the pupils in the Grosse Rue were also known to him, some being intimate friends. When in 1614 he went to Liége to open a Jesuit house of studies—theology and philosophy—he already knew and approved of Mary Ward's plans; and in 1616, before many Jesuits had become reconciled to her ideas, it was perhaps Father Gerard who invited her to open a house of her new Institute in Liége, where he became the friend and lifelong champion of Mary and her Institute.

But before this consoling development, the English Ladies had to pass through various vicissitudes, the chief of these being Mary's health, which remained delicate in spite of the speedy recovery through Our Lady's intercession in 1611. A short address by Father Lee to the community early in 1612 shows his friendly attitude: "Now, children, you see that it is necessary for God's honour, that your Superior seek some means to get her health, and as she hath given you all satisfaction, so it is thought necessary that another Superior be chosen amongst you, that she, having her health restored, may continue her care of you. . . . Sister Barbara Babthorpe is to be Superior, and nevertheless to have a particular care over you in the noviceship." From now until his death Father Lee never wavered in his care and solicitude for Mary and her Institute, and we reluctantly omit the spiritual and fatherly discourses with which he encouraged the young community. In 1614 we find him so solidly in their favour that he is in a group taking steps to present the plans for their Institute before the Holy See.

The leader of this group of friends was Bishop Blaise, who never at any time doubted the wisdom and the divine inspiration of the new Institute. One of the reasons, doubtless, that drew Mary to begin her work in St. Omer was her confidence in the bishop and her assurance that he trusted her. In the course of this story we shall see how practical was his good opinion of the English Ladies, defending them on every occasion against the injuries of calumniators.

Then there was the Infanta Isabella and her husband the Archduke Albert. Before settling at St. Omer, Mary had written and obtained their permission, given with what gladness we may well imagine. At this era, in all the large Flemish cities there was intense cultural activity; music, painting, architecture and the study of languages flourished in Brussels, Antwerp, Louvain and Liége and found generous patrons in Isabella and her husband. The great *conservatoires* in those cities in our day have here their origin, and the stream flowed on in the genius of a César Franck and an Ysaye. In painting, the name of Rubens stands out; there seemed no end to the canvases of glowing scenes and portraits that came from his studios in Antwerp, where his pupils worked with him; chief of these was, of course, Van Dyck. Rubens painted all the celebrities of his era, including Isabella and Albert, and was employed by them on diplomatic missions. In such an atmosphere of culture the request to open a school for English girls in St. Omer had received immediate compliance from the Infanta and her husband, especially as it was to be in charge of their friend Mary Ward. In the archives at Brussels there is still a letter from Mary to Isabella; it is dated October 1612, and reads:

Most Serene Lady,—Barbara Babthorpe, Anne Gage and Mary Ward declare that, seeing the necessities of the Catholics in England, and the difficulty they lie under of bringing up their children in the Catholic Faith, which cannot be done in that kingdom without great risk to the children and parents; and desiring to offer themselves to the service of God, for the education and instruction of such children as Catholics may wish to send to live in these States, they have settled themselves with other young English ladies in the town of St. Omer, where they have already received two nieces of the Earl of Shrewsbury and another young lady of the family of the Earl of Southampton; and they understand that many Catholic nobles intend to send their daughters to the said town to be brought up as Catholics under the care of the said ladies, in the Faith and good manners, in order that they may either be Religious in these parts, or, returning to marry in England, may there maintain what here they have learned. . . .

The memorial ends by asking the protection and favour of her Most Serene Highness. When the commotion over non-enclosure reached Isabella's ears, she must have wondered why anyone could not see that enclosure would be quite unsuitable for an Institute with such a programme. Never once in the whole course of Mary's troubles did this princess fail her; and when Mary on her travels would call to see her at the court in Brussels, all business was put aside while she attended to her much-loved guest.

By 1616 there were sixty nuns in the Institute, six of whom

were permanently in the London house, where Mary had installed Susanna Rookwood as Superior in 1614. In spite of her own health Mary crossed the Channel every year to England, remaining there for the greater part of 1614 and 1615. While there, they wore secular dress and carried on their apostolate among all classes, giving valuable help to the priests in preparing people for baptism and the other sacraments. . . . Returning to St. Omer in 1615, Mary, on the advice of Bishop Blaise and Father Lee, drew up a document showing the form of her Institute, so that it might be sent to Pope Paul V. She was in a few months to face the sorrow of the death of her good friend, Father Lee, who in spite of his failing health had done much for the good name of Mary and her Institute by sympathetic reports to the Jesuit houses in St. Omer and Rome.

The petition of the English Virgins which was laid at the feet of Paul V is a well-drawn-up document in Latin, containing a sketch of the spirit and object of the projected Institute. The grievous state of heretical England is the moving cause of the undertaking; and to aid as far as women can in the great work of its conversion is the object laid down. There is no mention of any name for the Institute, nor of any proposal to use the Rule of St. Ignatius. The reply from Paul V was most favourable: Bishop Blaise was commanded to take on himself their chief care and protection. The letter ends with the promise that if they continue in their holy way of living and their good work, "the Apostolic See will also deliberate about confirming their Institute."

A measure of stability now being given to their status, applicants for admission to the novitiate greatly increased in numbers, thus making a filiation in another city a matter of necessity. Conditions being propitious, it was to Liége that Mary turned her steps. Her health being so unsatisfactory, religious friends strongly recommended her to take a course of the health waters at Spa—"taking the waters" being a recognized cure in past centuries for many physical ills. The foundation at nearby Liége was to follow; so it was with some excitement that the community packed up for Mary and her companions (Barbara Ward, Barbara Babthorpe, and we know not what others). Mary said her good-byes to the children in the class-rooms, recommending them to put their minds on their Latin translations and to be very particular to speak only in French at their French recreations; the girls smiled back at their dear Mother Mary Ward, though some did look a trifle guilty at the mention of French conversation—it was so much easier to tell jokes in good, witty English. But they appreciated the education and culture that was in the very atmosphere of the school; they promised Mother that they would have ready for her return their new Italian songs, arranged in four parts. Oh yes, they would pray for her! Their young faces showed their affection as she turned at the door to smile and bow. "Good-bye, Mother, good-bye."

As the assembled community of nearly sixty nuns took their places in the community room for a farewell conference, they thought with some pride of the projected house in Liége. The London filiation had taken place gradually and as a matter of course. The Liége affair was different—more exciting: and the Institute had been in existence only seven years. All of these nuns were young, and already in imagination they saw the journey: the halt at Brussels, the short sojourn at the court of Albert and Isabella; then the waters at Spa (imaginations

played round here for a space) and the arrival at Liége, where
the bishop was Prince Ferdinand, the brother of Maximilian I,
of Bavaria. . . . But all distractions away! Mother Mary
Ward had taken her place at the head of the table and had
begun to speak:

My dear Sisters,—I know that you do not need any reminder from
me to ask God that I may do only His will in this new venture.
For it would be very foolish of us to desire anything however
good it may appear, apart from the fulfilment of the Divine Will.
Whether we go abroad or stay at home we ought to make a sanctuary of our hearts. Let us love solitude and fly, as much as we can,
unnecessary conversation with seculars. It is impossible to serve
God and the world at the same time, for our dear Lord says, "He
who is not with Me is against Me." It is well for us to remember
that. . . . Let us work and suffer for God; and, for the rest, let
Him make use of us according to His good pleasure; for the fulfilment of His most holy Will should be our sole wish and only desire. Let us pray for each other that we may love our vocation,
prizing and loving it above all other ways of living, for Our Lord
has said in the Gospel that he who keeps and teaches the Commandments shall be great in the Kingdom of Heaven. . . . Things
will often be difficult. But it very ill becomes a religious person to
be fainthearted; for she knows well that God is omnipotent, and
that He loves her infinitely, and therefore will permit nothing that
could hurt her. . . . Let us not grumble about anything. We
should be ashamed to say that anything appears hard to us in the
service of God, for to those who love all is light. It should be impossible for us to be sad; and while we seek after true and heroic
virtues we should banish from us all signs of sadness, and take care
to show always a cheerful temperament. In our calling, a cheerful
mind, a good understanding and a great desire after virtue are
necessary; but of all these a cheerful mind is the most so. . . .

Mary then spoke of her great desire that charity should be the distinguishing mark of the community—a charity built on respect for each other:

Ours should be as courteous towards each other as if they were strangers, but at the same time as gentle and amiable as they are accustomed to be with their most intimate friends. . . .[2]

The farewells over, the travellers set out on foot—Oh those terrible journeys on foot, in all weathers, on all kinds of roads! Winefrid seemed to see them in all their roughness as she pressed her cheek to Mary's at the moment of good-bye. She and Mary were the one age—almost thirty-one; girlhood friends drawn still closer by the strong, sweet bonds of religious life. Winefrid whispers a few strict injunctions to the two Barbaras concerning Mary's rest and food. And the journey begins—nothing so interesting and romantic as the young nuns pictured. Isabella was kind; but the roads were bad, and feet ached, and one grew hungry and thirsty and depressed and wondered how it was all going to turn out at Liége. Well, it turned out well—very well. Father Gerard was helpful and kind; and the Prince-Bishop Ferdinand, though away from Liége at the time, sent a gracious message of welcome. A community was set up and a school opened. All went without a hitch, so that Mary wrote in her journal: "O my Lord, how liberal are You and how rich are they to whom You will vouchsafe to be a friend." But Mary was never carried away by success, nor would she allow the community in Liége to be over-sanguine. Within a short time they were to remember her words: "Whoever will serve God according to her state in this Institute must of necessity love the Cross, and be ready to suffer much for Christ's sake."

[2] This conference is compiled from Mary Ward's maxims.

In the early summer of 1617 Mary was again in England with fresh members for the growing community there. It was indeed a difficult life for them. Hardly would they have settled in one house and organized their work, visiting the poor or the prisoners suffering for their faith, when spies would set pursuivants on their tracks. Flight was often the only effective sort of tactics. Mary's visits back and forth had not gone unnoticed, and it was pretty well recognized among the Protestant persecutors that her house was a shelter for priests and a centre of operations for conversions. She must have been indeed very well known by repute, for Abbot, the Archbishop of Canterbury, is reported to have said: "That woman has done more harm than many priests"; he went on to say that he would exchange six or seven Jesuits for her. A description of her appearance was circulated, at his command, among pursuivants who were ordered to find and seize her. Mary's friends were distressed and alarmed as the danger seemed to close in round her; they begged her to go back to St. Omer. She went; the chronicler adds as a further reason that Father Gerard in Liége was suggesting that now was the time to open a novitiate in that city.

An interlude at St. Omer must be fitted in. It appears that one day when Mr. Sackville was chatting with the Jesuit Fathers at the College after his return from seeing Pope Paul V on Mary's behalf, he told the Fathers that the Cardinals thought well of the plan of the English Ladies. This called forth from one of the priests the cynical observation: "It is true whilst they are in their first fervour; but fervour will decay, and when all is done they are but women!" The remark was repeated to the Ladies, who were so angry that they did not know what steps to take to show their displeasure.

They were women of prayer, but that did not crush their high spirits. The rule of silence was difficult to keep during those days, as young nuns longed to whisper to each other: "I wish Mother were home!"

Well, there was Mother at last. And what did she do when she was told the churlish remark? She assembled the community and gave them one of the most dignified and inspiring allocutions any foundress has ever made to her nuns. She spoke first of fervour:

Fervour is a will to do good, that is, a preventing grace of God, and a gift given gratis by God, which we do not merit. It is true fervour doth many times grow cold; but what is the cause? Is it because we are women? No; but because we are *imperfect* women. There is no such difference between men and women. . . . Fervour is not placed in feelings, but in a will to do well, which women may have as well as men. Women may do great things, as we have seen by example of many saints who have done great things. And I hope in God it will be seen that women in time to come will do much. . . . This is truth, this is verity; to do what we have to do, well. Many think it nothing to do ordinary things. But for us it is. To do ordinary things well, to keep our constitutions . . . this is for us, and this by God's grace will maintain fervour. . . .

It was a long speech, the "verity" speech, as it came to be called; and by the time Mary ended, her sisters were solaced and inspired to go forward in their course, their Superior communicating to them her strength of purpose. Who among them ever forgot her closing words: "This is all I have to say at this time: that you love verity and truth"?

But it was to go to Liége that she had returned from England; so on she went. There she met personally the Prince-Bishop, who was on most friendly terms with the English

Ladies in Liége. Mary especially pleased him by the care she took that everything connected with the church, the saying of Office and all the ritual, should be done according to the Roman rite. The singing of the nuns at Mass and Divine Office gave him much pleasure, and he frequently said Mass in their convent chapel. Before leaving Liége Mary made the Spiritual Exercises under the direction of Father Gerard, who was henceforth to be her close friend and adviser. In some of her notes during this retreat we see a little of her inner life. She seemed to have a premonition of a great loneliness that would come on her: "I offered myself to suffer with love and gladness whatsoever trouble should happen in my doing of His will. . . . Perchance there was some great trouble to happen about the confirmation of our Institute. . . . I offered myself willingly to this difficulty, and besought Our Lord with tears that He would give me grace to bear it. . . . I saw there was no help nor comfort for me but to cleave fast to Him; and so I did, for He was there to help me. . . ."

But England was calling her again; and it was with great relief that Susanna Rookwood and her community welcomed her to London in 1618. Inwardly they may have feared for her safety, but she inspired them to such courage from her own stores that they put their fears out the door. No priest who saw them working for souls in London would ever be so anti-feminist as to say: "They are but women." No threats could keep Mary away from the state prisons where priests were held in the most wretched surroundings. They were often half-starved; yet they managed to say Mass in secret, helped by the money which Mary and her company used for bribing the gaolers. No, the Jesuits in the Wisbeach prison would not have said, "They are but women."

All during these months the pursuivants of Abbot, the Archbishop, were hunting for Mary, who seemed to walk unscathed through all dangers. Hearing that Abbot had said he would like to see her, she announced one day that she intended to call on him at Lambeth Palace. Winefrid and Barbara, in whom she confided, were horrified, but when she persisted they said with as great determination that they would go with her. In bright taffeta gowns and stylish ruffs, they set off. . . . See them now in the Archbishop's study as the footman patiently awaits their pleasure in the hall, after telling these charming ladies that the Archbishop is not at home. Mary slips a diamond ring from her finger and scratches on the window pane *Mary Ward*—her card for the Archbishop!

There is something of the adventurous Renaissance spirit in Mary Ward. It led her into astonishing situations; but in the visit to Lambeth Palace we discern, surely, a genuine love for the soul of her enemy. She knew the power God had given her for influencing people, and it is very likely that she thought Abbot might be led to practise at least some degree of humanity and chivalry when confronted with three ladies who trusted to his qualities of a gentleman. But divine providence arranged that this episcopal upstart should not be required to behave as a gentleman. It was better so.

By now Mary was making plans to go back to St. Omer. One soul was holding her back: a priest who had given up saying Mass and was sliding downhill into wickedness. He belonged to a good family, but conditions were too much for him, and he at first received Mary's kind solicitude with ill-humour. In prayer and penance she besought the Lord to give her this soul that she might return it to Him. She went to any fashionable gathering where she thought she would meet him. Then, one day, grace broke the icy casing round his heart; he made a good confession and took up his priestly duties again. . . . Mary put her things together and went off to catch the boat to Dunkirk. She and the priest both embarked, but the boat was driven back into the port by the high winds. What happened to him we do not know, but the pursuivants closed in on Mary, took her prisoner, and led her back to London, where she was brought at once before a judge at the Guildhall.

Knowing well that to have a rosary was an offence punishable by loss of property or perpetual imprisonment, Mary nevertheless drew hers from her pocket and wound it round her fingers. Seeing it, one of the judges uttered some blasphemy, calling forth from Mary a courageous reproof. Looking him in the eye she said in forthright Yorkshire style: "What! A miserable man, a good-for-nothing wretch, is to blaspheme and revile the most holy and divine Mother, the Queen and Lady of all creatures!" She was at once sent to prison. When she arrived at the door she knelt down and kissed the threshold, oblivious of guards around her. They, for their part, were so awe-struck by her calm demeanour that they treated her with the utmost respect. She had every reason to believe that she was facing martyrdom, and her hours of contemplative prayer in prison remind us of St. Thomas More, whose lights in prayer made almost a heaven of his dungeon. But Winefrid and Barbara and the others who came to see her were by no means reconciled to the idea of revering her as a martyr, though their hearts were almost without hope when they were told that sentence of death had been passed on her. However, even Archbishop Abbot's fanaticism had lucid moments. A contemporary letter says: "Sentence of death was passed upon her for religion, but there was no execution for fear of odium."

Before we let Mary get away to St. Omer there is one incident that must be told. It completes the story of the priest and is the subject of a picture in the *Painted Life*. The inscription runs: "As Mary was once earnestly praying for a priest whom she had withdrawn from a bad life (in fear lest he might have met with an evil chance) God showed to her visibly his holy Guardian Angel standing at the top of his bedstead, lovingly stretching out his arms over him, as if he would shelter him from all danger. Who said to her, 'Seest thou how faithfully I guard him?' " This was one of her heavenly moments as she sat on her pallet in the prison cell. From then till the end of her life she could summon to her memory the form of that celestial visitant whom she called always the "Fine Good Angel."

Finally Mary sailed for Dunkirk. She was not to see England again for over twenty years.

11. Schools in Rome, Naples and Perugia

> *"Winning ways, airs innocent, maiden man-*
> *ners, sweet locks, loose locks, long locks,*
> *lovelocks, gaygear, going gallant, girl-*
> *grace—"*
>
> (GERARD MANLEY HOPKINS)

By 1620 Mary realized that she had other enemies besides the persecutors of her faith in England. After all, she had opened her eyes in infancy to a life where pursuivants were an accepted hazard, much as hot ashes would be to people living near an active volcano. Until she came to St. Omer at the age of twenty-one, her whole life had been conditioned by the Penal Laws; and when she visited England she met their ferocity with true Renaissance zest. But the whispering campaign among Catholics in Flanders was a hurtful thing as she felt its malice slowly developing. Letters were coming from Catholics in England—Catholics who had never met her—to tell the Jesuits in Flanders that her Institute was a cause of discord in Jesuit houses in England—some being for her, others against her. In St. Omer itself, Bishop Blaise already had to defend her against charges made by secular priests living in exile from England. They complained that the English Ladies influenced and prevailed on girls to enter their novitiate, even though the girls wanted to go to the Benedictines and others. In a strong letter, Bishop Blaise disposed of this charge by giving the numbers of English girls who had visited the English Ladies at St. Omer and then gone on to other novitiates.

We must state and face the unpleasant fact that the disunity of English Catholics, at a period when unity would have meant so much, was a tragedy. We can explain, and surely excuse, the disunity by pointing to almost a hundred years of bitter persecution. It gave the Church martyrs and confessors, but those who remained received injuries to their personality, becoming in many cases harassed and suspicious. The really sad element in this disunity was that they were all ready to lay down their lives for the faith, but they were not ready to live on a supernatural level of charity with their fellow-Catholics. The most serious manifestation of this was the ill-feeling between the Jesuits and the secular clergy.

The chief difference of opinion was on the subject of the restoration of the hierarchy to England; the unfortunate secular priests feeling the need of bishops, the Jesuits feeling that the times were not yet propitious for such a move.

But grievous as all this was to Mary, it lacked the sharp tooth of the malice that showed itself among her own nuns. *This* was something she could not at first believe; she was so trusting and above-board herself that a plotter in any of her communities was a calamity not to be thought of. The trouble began in one of the houses of Liége. (A second house had been opened there.) Jealousy seems to have been the motive, and the name of Mary Allcock must ever remain a reminder of the depths to which an originally generous character can fall. It began with ill-natured criticism of Mary Ward; calumny soon followed, and Mary Allcock, finding a few disaffected nuns in the Liége community, communicated her poisonous suspicions not only inside the community but where they could do the maximum of harm. An old manuscript endorsed "Godfather's Information" in the archives of the Westminster Diocese contained accounts of Mary's extravagance—and worse—communicated "by Mrs. Mary Allcock the first Mother Minister of Mrs. Warde's company at Leodes (Liége)."

"When she travelleth she is extraordinary jovial, and (to the Mother Minister's grief) most lavish in expenses both at home and abroad." In England Mary and the others had worn the latest "phantastical" mode—yellow ruffs just introduced. Barbara Ward had been seen besides "in a bright taffeta gown and rich petticoats, trimmed of the newest fashion." Visiting the prisons they had been so "prodigal" as to give "each keeper (who wished more such guests) an angel apiece." Moreover "At Knightsbridge, an infamous place," they had lived with "vanitie and riot . . . and the waites (I mean the musicians) came from London to salute her night by night, and received the reward of two shillings every time."

Poor Mary, obliged to safeguard her prison visits by these disguises, so attractive as still to draw unwelcome attention, how little did she imagine the stories told in all innocence to the Liége community being thus transformed, with the addition that—on her return—"her manner was to be feasted for three days successively, the first night an extraordinary great banquet."

Few things did more harm to Mary's cause than "Godfather's Information."

In the year 1620 with which we began this chapter there were two more flourishing houses, one at Cologne, the other at Trèves, both foundations being helped considerably by funds collected by Father Gerard from his friends. All the money went into the building and furnishing of the schools, as Mary and her companions lived in great personal poverty. That did not save them from one calumny which circulated though scotched again and again—that they travelled about as wealthy women, spending lavishly in entertainments. And now the sudden removal, by order of the General, of Father Gerard from the office of Rector of Liége, because of his generous help, left Mary in no doubt as to her standing in the opinion of the General of the Jesuits. Often at prayer she would put her hands over her eyes in defence against the thought of the final words in the heavenly communication of 1611: "Father General will never permit it. Go to him."

There were thus many reasons why she should go to Rome at once and personally confer with Pope Paul V about her Institute. She must hasten; he was old and might die. Also, she had lately met the saintly Carmelite Father Domenico di Gesù Maria, who was to remain one of her champions for life; he urged her to go to Rome without delay. As she had dreaded, Pope Paul V did die, early in 1621, to be succeeded by Gregory XV, old and in failing health but with a great appreciation of Father Domenico. So with good hopes of success Mary made her preparations for the journey—a journey on foot across Europe, with the ever present possibility of an encounter with soldiers, for the terrible Thirty Years' War had broken out three years earlier. However, Mary and her companions planned her route to avoid hostile ground by going through the provinces of Southern Germany and Switzerland; and in winter when soldiers would be in winter quarters.

As preparations went forward in St. Omer a well-built boy of about nineteen called and asked to see the Superior. He was Robert Wright, whose father had been involved in the Gunpowder Plot and killed in the capture.[1] Robert was Mary Ward's first cousin, and at this time had just finished his school

[1] See chapter 7.

days at the College in St. Omer. He had often visited Mary during his days there, and she had told him about her plans for the conversion of England. Hearing that she was on the point of going to Rome, he decided to ask her to take him as a serving-man: he felt he had no vocation to be a priest, but he would like to devote his life to God by saving souls. Here, then, was the opportunity. His boyish face showed his embarrassment as he explained himself to Mary; he hated talking about himself and his ideals. Mary relieved his mind at once by saying that he was just the kind of person she needed, and that of course he could accompany her party to Rome. Thus began for Robert a life of unselfish devotion to the Institute; during Mary's lifetime he accompanied her on all her trips, effacing himself completely to act as a serving-man. True, generous Robert Wright!

Another devoted companion of the Institute as Mary travelled back and forth across Europe was Father Henry Lee, nephew of Father Roger Lee whose championship of Mary he seemed to inherit. He acted as chaplain on these trips.

With another serving-man (Mary hesitated to throw all the menial work of seeing to the packhorse and luggage on to Robert), the party was ready to set out on October 21, 1621. Besides the three men, there were Mary, Winefrid, Barbara Ward, Mary Poyntz and one we have not met before, Margaret Horde. There was also a lay-sister with them. As the way led through Brussels, there was a call made on the Infanta Isabella, who had been for some time encouraging Mary to make the Roman trip. She now gave her two letters to help her when she went for her audience to Pope Gregory: one from Isabella's brother, the King of Spain, the other from the Emperor Ferdinand (not the bishop). Isabella wrote also with her own hand to the Pope. In the practical matter of suitable dress for the journey she was a competent adviser, saying No to the idea of walking across Europe in simple out-door raiment. A pilgrim's outfit of cloak and staff and high beaver hat was what each should have, so that they would be readily received at inns and given along the highways the respect that pilgrims still enjoyed. So the Ladies left Brussels looking much more imposing than when they entered it, and fared forth on a journey that was to last two months. One of the three places where they rested—a day at each—was the village containing the Holy House of Loreto.

The morning after their arrival they rose in the early hours to be at the shrine for the first Mass at 3 A.M. Mary spent there the whole day in prayer; she asked Our Lady to obtain for her light and strength to go forward in the work which God had given her to do. In her soul she received an answer: that her portion would be to labour and suffer for Christ. She embraced her lonely destiny, even accepting with love a showing that must have made her tremble: that a great deal of her suffering would come from the Sovereign Pontiff himself. That memory must have haunted her for many weeks after she found herself in Rome. Now, on Christmas Eve 1621, when the travellers saw etched against the skyline in the chilly winter sun Michelangelo's dome crowning St. Peter's Basilica, and the spires and campaniles of Rome, Mary fell on her knees, rendering submission to the Successors of St. Peter in the Holy See. That was to be, symbolically, her attitude to the Papacy all her life.

The pilgrims made their way at once to St. Peter's, where Mary wished to pray at the tomb of the Apostle, the first Pope. The streets and squares were full of gay crowds celebrating Christmas Eve. (Little they knew here of silent bells and

desecrated sanctuaries.) But they answered the pilgrims' en-
quiries with kindness and helpful courtesy, directing them to
St. Peter's. The imposing Baroque façade was fresh from the
hands of Maderna and his workmen, after the finishing touches
seven years before. Bernini, only twenty-three, was still
dreaming of his works—each to be a masterpiece. In St. Peter's
alone there were to be the *baldacchino*, the tombs, and, outside,
the glorious colonnades. Even before possessing these works
the basilica was a treasury of art. In the square was the tall
Egyptian obelisk, set up there in the year of Mary's birth. But
we very much doubt if, on this first visit, she saw anything as
she passed, tired and footsore, through the festive crowds to
the tomb of St. Peter, where she remained some time in prayer.
The next place to be visited, and immediately, was the tomb
of St. Ignatius in the church of the Gesù. She knew that he
would know why she was anxious about the outcome of this
Roman journey.

One of the first of her friends to get in touch with her was
Father Domenico di Gesù, who had arrived in Rome only a
fortnight earlier. Because of his influence with Pope Gregory
XV he was able to arrange an early audience for Mary; so on
St. Stephen's Day she was again in St. Peter's before being led
in to the Papal Palace of the Vatican. That a woman, even
though a friend of princes, should be pleading her own cause
in a personal interview with the Pope was a novelty that would
please few churchmen of that era. But Isabella's letter and the
personal influence with the Pope of Father Domenico greatly
smoothed Mary's path for this first interview.

Pope Gregory received her with much kindness, asking her
questions about her work and listening intently to her account
of life in England under the Penal Laws. He seemed to ap-

preciate at once the need for women in the work of its conversion. He asked Mary to put in writing her plans for her
Institute, so that he might study them, and dismissed her with
a fatherly blessing. She left much consoled. She would have
been even happier had she known that the Pope was to write
immediately to Isabella that "Mary's piety is highly to be
praised, which has with such labour gathered together a band
of companions whom she brings forward and offers for God's
honour. . . ." He added: "As the letter of your Highness
contains such an excellent testimony of all her virtues, we desire
that her piety and this commendation should be weighed with
no little favour, and have therefore commanded that her Institute and her motives should be immediately taken into consideration."

The second visit Mary had to pay was to the Father General
of the Jesuits, Father Vitelleschi, whose attitude to her Institute she knew was one of suspicion. The removal of Father
Gerard from the office of Rector in Liége because of his material support, and the recent instructions the General had
given to the Jesuits in England "to forbid any of Ours to teach
catechism in their schools"—all this was known to Mary, and
gave her no good hope of a pleasant interview. As she went to
meet him she revolved in her mind the two points she wished
to stress: first, that she must abide at all costs with her decision
to adopt the rules of St. Ignatius; second, that she had no intention of asking his Society to have any responsibility in her
Institute. At this distance from events, we wonder that she
should have had to labour the points; for the greater number of
women's religious congregations today have the Rule of St.
Ignatius adapted for women. But in the seventeenth century

the idea was new, and (being new) repugnant to an anti-feminist world.

We have no report of the interview, but whatever Father Vitelleschi thought of her plans, he treated her and her companions with much courtesy and kindness during the whole of their sojourn in Rome. Their lives of holiness and their record of heroic friendship with persecuted Jesuits in England demanded at least that. In connection with the aloofness of the General with regard to Mary's plans, an ironic position may be observed: that the chief ground of the dislike felt for her by the agents in Rome of the secular clergy was what she was a tool of the Jesuits! The Pope must have been bewildered by the strange reports in her regard that became part of his official correspondence every day. With words of warning from all sides, it is not to be wondered that he paused before confirming this Institute which threatened to excite Catholics almost to another schism.

As the weeks passed, Mary realized that the Pope was less willing to confirm the Institute than he had been at their meeting. She took then what all her friends said was the wisest course: she got permission from the Pope to open a free school in Rome,[2] so that he and the Cardinals (among whom she was becoming a subject of contradiction) might see the usual way of life of the English Ladies. Once having decided on this course, Mary secured a large house and sent to Liége asking Barbara Babthorpe to bring some of the community to staff the school, to which the young girls of Rome were soon flocking. Roman parents, who had been discussing the English Ladies ever since their arrival the previous Christmas, were

[2] Free schools for boys had recently been opened by St. Joseph Calasanctius.

delighted when the school opened—children usefully occupied all day, and no fees! Citizens who had looked askance at the Ladies in their black dresses, white wimple, white band across the forehead and white cuffs, began to accept the phenomenon of religious who did not have to live behind their grille. These kind and charming English Ladies, to whom the lively Roman girls ran with trust and affection, soon won appreciations from cardinals, priests and parents. Even the wicked gave testimony, saying openly that if such schools continued, the evil houses in Rome would go to ruin.

It was at this time that Mary met one of her greatest personal sorrows, the death of her faithful and loving sister Barbara from some kind of wasting disease following an epidemic of small-pox. The sisters (Oblates of St. Frances of Rome) at the Torre dei Specchi, to whom Mary had been introduced by Father Domenico shortly after her arrival, had been so kind as to invite Barbara and a companion to live with the community at the Torre dei Specchi so that they might quickly learn Italian. The two English Ladies had gone back to their own community before the outbreak of the epidemic. When that had passed and it was seen that Barbara's health had been undermined, the Oblates had her back with them, hoping to nurse her back to health. Their charity was one of the few bright spaces of those days in Mary's life. But Barbara was not to get well, so she returned to her own community to die. The two sisters had hardly been a day separated since they began life in St. Omer in 1609, Barbara being the first to offer in the sharing of every hardship, and accompanying her on every journey—always so witty and sympathetic, smoothing out difficulties with her gifts of tact and self-sacrifice. Now she was dying. During her delirious hours Mary sat by her bed, listen-

ing with breaking heart to her disjointed talk—mostly of childhood days at Newby: the peacock on the stone wall near the
orchard, the swans on the lake. . . . And the tears ran down
Mary's cheeks, though she thought that tears like those had
been quenched for ever. Outside, in the streets of Rome, the
snow was falling. It was the 25th of January, 1623.

The days preceding and following Barbara's death showed
the friendship of the Jesuits living at the Gesù, where a notice
in the sacristy for weeks stated the command of the Father
General that Barabara should be remembered in the Masses of
all the priests. When her death was announced he ordered all
Masses to be said in the Jesuit colleges in Rome for the repose
of her soul. Father Gerard[3] was in Rome at this time, having arrived a week or so before Barbara's death.

The Father General, having learned at first hand the worth
of Mary's character, evidently now viewed the Liége collaboration in a different light, for he seems to have approved of
the many Jesuits in Rome who openly showed friendship for
Mary and her Institute. Being aware of this, it was a comfort
to her to confer with Father Gerard about her work. She
must certainly have consulted him and obtained his approval
on her plan of founding a house in Naples. There she would
be judged on the merits of her life and work and on nothing
else; whereas in Rome partisan feeling ran high. Mary longed
to open a school away from all the turmoil of controversy
and the uneasiness of knowing that even a cardinal had spies
watching the comings and goings of her sisters. So, without
friends or letters or money (except the pittance for food on

[3] In a note to his autobiography republished in English in 1951, we read
that "in 1622 he visited Rome to get papal support for the new Institute of
Religious Women founded by Mary Ward."

the way), she set out on foot across the country for Naples. Winefrid Wigmore was with her, and Susanna Rookwood to be the Superior, and Margaret Genison (a niece of Father Gerard), besides others; and of course Father Henry Lee and faithful Robert. It was May 12, 1623. Being so poor, they went to cheap and insanitary lodgings from which they soon had to move on account of an illness which seized Mary. One of the Jesuits of the college in Naples, knowing from letters from Father Gerard of their journey thither, sought them out and obtained the loan of a house in a healthy quarter; but it was unfurnished—nothing but bare walls—so that Mary had to stretch her tired and sick body on a pallet of straw on the floor. The priest coming to see her was so horrified at her plight that he hastened to a lady known to him and asked her to send Mary a bedstead and mattress. So began the house in Naples.

The Jesuits gave them introductions to the parents of their pupils whose sisters were until then schooled at home. Those homes, with façades on to the handsome streets, were like palaces—many had been palaces of some once powerful families. In the newer houses the Baroque spirit ran riot round the preposterously ornate staircases and out the doorways flanked by statues. Here, four caryatides upheld the cornice of a doorway; there, a fabulous monster opened its stone mouth to receive the postman's letters.[4] But teen-age girls in Naples had a dull enough time until they went to the school of the English Ladies, who came like a wind from the north to break in on the Baroque stuffiness of their restricted lives.

The summer sun beat down on those streets all day long, and the blinds were drawn against the glare. There were no gardens or shady trees, but there were fountains—fountains every-

[4] Described in *Southern Baroque* by Sacheverell Sitwell.

where. They splashed and gurgled in every stone-paved square, tempering the heat with their rippling coolness. Mary and her companions made friends, rested, prayed and waited. In July news came of the death of Pope Gregory, and Mary was torn between the desire to return to Rome, to attend to the interests of the Institute, and the feeling that she should stay in Naples at least until the school could open. But as usual she showed nothing of her anxiety to her community, strengthening them by saying gently: "We must so wholly devote ourselves to the Divine Will, that we are as it were enclosed in it, and therefore cannot on any side withdraw from it."

At the end of August the summer seemed to come to a sudden end. Each day for weeks rain hung like a grey veil over the Bay and shrouded the summit of Vesuvius—a perpetual wonder to the sisters as they gazed at it through their community-room window. It was not till the end of September that the school could open. When Mary saw that things were promising well, she left Winefrid Wigmore to conduct any business with ecclesiastical and civil powers in her name and returned to Rome, where the chief interest in every conversation was the coming election of the new pope. Cardinal Maffeo Barberini was elected and became Pope Urban VIII. Patron of the arts, his name will always be linked with the name of Bernini, whose work is still one of the chief glories of St. Peter's. Their collaboration may be gathered from a statement reported to have been made by Urban to Bernini: "It is good fortune for you, Cavaliere, to see as Pope Cardinal Maffeo Barberini; but greater is our good fortune that Cavalier Bernini lives in our Pontificate."[5] He came from an old princely Roman family, and piety was not lacking in his many-sided character, as we

5 Quoted in *Rome* by Edward Hutton.

may see from his first reported act after his election; he knelt in the Sistine Chapel and asked God that he should die at once if his election were to prove hurtful to the Church. Even accepting this report, it is surely not disrespectful to surmise that, with all his cultural interests, the plans of an English lady for the conversion of her country must have seemed a remote business.

While Mary was trying to obtain an audience with Pope Urban, she received an invitation from the Bishop of Perugia to make a foundation in that town. She accepted, but deferred and deferred the actual journey, until she saw there was no hope of an immediate audience with the Pope. Packets of gold coins sent from Naples to the Roman house every few weeks (and received with what gratitude) showed that affairs were going well there and encouraged Mary to set off for Perugia. Her letter from there on February 6, 1624, shows the warmth of the Bishop's welcome, with its practical provision for a school, and the enthusiasm of the townspeople, "who are superabundant in their compliments and their discourse not only eloquent but of such continuance" that it was difficult to see them off the premises by 6 P.M. . . . The schools went well, but the Cross was never far away in Mary's life. Word came of the death of her dear Susanna Rookwood, Superior at Naples, and Mary herself now became the victim of an internal illness that never left her. So ill was she that friends recommended the waters at San Cassiano, in the mountains about seventy miles distant from Perugia and a few miles south of Florence. Taking the waters also was Cardinal Trescio from Rome; he was very ill, and his life was despaired of. Mary, hearing this (she had recovered a good deal), set off walking on a pilgrimage to a shrine of Our Lady on Monte Giovino.

She obtained the immediate cure of the Cardinal, who hearing of Mary's pilgrimage on his behalf became her staunch friend. He was not among the cardinals who were to deliberate on her affairs.

After returning to Rome, Mary at last secured an audience with the Pope, who called together a congregation of four cardinals to examine her plans. As the one great object of her solicitude was her own country-people, she confined her application for confirmation to the members of the Institute in England, Flanders and Germany. But on non-inclosure and the other points she remained firm. She did not perhaps fully realize that she was single-handed against a custom that was not to be breached for another two hundred years. But she did realize that she was entering a valley of extreme loneliness, for she wrote to Winefrid: "I think, dear child, the trouble and long loneliness is not far from me, which whensoever it is, happy success will follow."

12. Holy Year: Schools Closed in Rome

"Hold the high way, and let thy soul thee lead,
And truth shall deliver...."

(CHAUCER)

THE HOLY Year of 1625 opened with joyful celebrations on the Christmas Eve of 1624 in the four Roman basilicas. Pope Urban opened the Holy Door at St. Peter's while Cardinal Mellino performed a similar ceremony at Sta. Maria Maggiore, where Mary and her companions from the Roman house were among the throng of worshippers. They were probably the only ones to remain there in prayer until the dawn. During this first sojourn in Rome, as well as during those visits to follow, Sta. Maria Maggiore was their special church. It contains the miraculous picture, now the special Madonna of the Institute, known as St. Luke's Madonna. Whether it was actually painted by St. Luke is of little moment. Pope Paul V thought so highly of it that he had a special chapel, the Capella Borghese, built for it at the basilica. The history of the picture goes back to the sixth century when, during the ravages of a plague, the Pope (St. Gregory the Great) carried it in procession from Sta. Maria Maggiore to St. Peter's, while he heard angelic hosts singing the *Regina Coeli*. Mary Ward and her companions singled it out as their special picture, renewing their vows each year before it, putting themselves particularly under the protection of Our Lady of the Snows, in whose honour the basilica was built, or at least converted from its pagan origins, in the fifth century. In the Basilica of Sta. Maria Maggiore, so hallowed by the Christian centuries, our Institute may be said to have its spiritual roots.

Mary Ward had great need of the graces of the Holy Year, for before Easter approached she knew almost for certain that not only was the confirmation of her Institute to be refused, but her schools were to be closed. So great was the dread which she inspired in the hearts of the agents of the English secular clergy that they set a strong movement on foot to urge the Pope to expel her and hers from Rome. But in this they did not succeed; and it must be conceded that even had they not shown such enmity it was unlikely that the Pope or the College of Cardinals were ready to accept her novel ideas of a Religious Institute. The safest course, it seemed to them, for the present was to close the schools, at least in Rome where conflicting opinions were exasperating even the most patient churchmen. To show how little it was a personal matter, we mention that one of the many noble Roman ladies who at this time were showing themselves friendly to Mary was the Princess Constanza Barberini, the Pope's sister-in-law. It must indeed have been a very puzzled Princess who heard a commotion of shouting and weeping in the street before her doors. (The Italian population do that kind of thing very well, though Mary, in a letter, excuses them by saying it was "contrary to their usual restraint.") The Princess was told that it was the "moaning and complaint" of the parents of the girls—and the girls themselves—at finding that the English Ladies were no longer allowed to have their schools. Troubled as the Princess must have been, we may excuse her for refraining from becoming embroiled in what she realized was a matter of Church policy; but her appreciation for Mary Ward increased, and she was able to prove her friendship for her within a few years.

The humiliation of finding herself and her work the subject of so much censure from high ecclesiastical authorities was a trial that Mary bore with touching equanimity. She remained serene and cheerful with her friends and was never heard to murmur or to blame anyone for the destruction of the work that had come to be almost her life. The deeper she went into the valley of humility, the more brightly did grace adorn her soul. The Holy Year was for her a year of tremendous graces in prayer. Every day, without once missing, she went to whatever church was holding the Quarant' Ore and spent long hours in prayer during the Exposition of the Blessed Sacrament. The *Painted Life* tells us of some of these graces: for instance, it recounts that between the 6th and 9th of April, while she was waiting for the decision of the cardinals, she was praying in the church of Sta. Maria dell'Orto, when she was so absorbed in the Divine Love that she was carried wholly out of herself in ecstasy, and, reposing in God alone, a clear sight was given to her of her own utter nothingness, and that God is All. Of another favour we give the wording of the *Painted Life*: "On the 26th of June of this year Mary received in the church of St. Eligius at Rome, before the Blessed Sacrament, such light and perception from God concerning the forgiveness of enemies, that she thereby acquired towards them a tone so tender as constantly to speak of them as the friends and purchasers of her heavenly reward." Hence the origin of the term "Jerusalem" given by the English Ladies among themselves to all those who were troubling and injuring them. (No doubt on the lips of those sisters not so richly endowed with grace as Mary was, the expression sometimes had an ironic edge.)

One other grace (there were several more than we mention) is concerned with the power of her intercessory prayer during this year of special devotions in the Quarant' Ore. A noted Catholic layman, Dr. Alphonso Ferro, whom Mary knew, was very ill with fever which parched his mouth and allowed him no sleep. Mary, visiting him and finding him in such a state, went at once to the Carmelite church near by, the church of the Madonna della Scala, where Quarant' Ore was being held. She petitioned Our Lady to obtain his cure, saying: "Give him my sleep; I will be content to want it." It was the Feast of Our Lady of the Rosary. That night the sick man slept untroubled, and his wife, who watched beside him, heard him say distinctly in his sleep: "O Signora! Oh what charity!" In the morning he awoke with joy, perfectly cured.

By the end of 1625 Mary saw that there was nothing to keep her in Rome during the present defeat of her plans, and her thoughts turned wistfully to England and Flanders. Though Mary Allcock continued to be a cause of dissension in Liége, Mary Ward enjoyed the continued confidence of the Prince-Bishop Ferdinand and the Apostolic Nuncio there. (Perhaps Mary Allcock had left the Institute but was still in the town; authors ought to be omniscient, but there are some things they do not know.) The confidence that those dignitaries still had in Mary Ward was shown by letters that they wrote to Rome, begging the congregation of cardinals sitting in judgment on Mary's work early in 1625 to consider the value of her plans. These letters did not prevent the closing of the schools, but they probably helped to establish Mary's personal reputation among cardinals who may have been wondering if the religious convulsions of Elizabethan England had thrown up a female Lollard. That is a mild surmise when put beside the aspersions of the clergy agents; but before we condemn them we have to remember that throughout the seventeenth century there was a widespread belief in witchcraft and that in England the last "witch" was condemned to death in 1712—almost a century after the period we are discussing.[1] Though the clergy agents scarcely believed that Mary was a witch, they could seriously put down in good Latin in their memorial to Pope Urban that "it is reasonably to be feared, if the reins be slackened to these women, that they will break out into various errors from want of sound and solid judgment, and be found to be sowers of false doctrines among the poor people." Cardinals sympathetic with the English Clergy possibly believed this.

What more could Mary do in the face of such opposition? She did the only thing: made preparations to leave Rome. Renewing her hours of prayer before the tabernacles in the various Roman churches, she was granted by God a premonition of the great suffering that was to come on herself and the Institute. One particular visit to the Blessed Sacrament is told in the *Painted Life:* "She was praying for the Institute in the church of St. Mark in Rome, when Almighty God impressed upon her mind the words of Our Lord, 'Can you drink of the chalice that I shall drink?' and immediately showed to her the great contradictions, persecutions and distresses which she should endure in the fulfilment of His holy will concerning it. She with joy offered herself to bear all."

[1] In England James I had statutes passed against witches, and, in 1768, John Wesley entered a solemn protest against people who disbelieved in witchcraft. He said it was like giving up the Bible. (See "Witchcraft" in *Chambers' Encyclopedia.*)

The only one in Rome with whom she could confer about her movements was Father Domenico. Father Gerard had been sent as Tertian Master to Ghent. Perhaps it was better so, for the Father General had grown more aloof from Mary's interests as a result of letters received from the Jesuit Provincial in England. In that country the hard-pressed clergy had been granted a bishop by the Pope; and the Jesuits, who had no wish to perpetuate any feud with them, were directed by their Provincial "to be ready to serve the Bishop for the good of souls" . . . and to be careful "to endeavour never to give him or the clergy any just occasion of offence." So, as has happened many times in human affairs, peace was made over "the dead body" of a third person who was an inconvenience. Regarding Mary and her companions, the English Jesuits were ordered by their Father General "not to meddle in their businesses, and make the world know that the Society hath no more to do with them, than with all other penitents who resort to them."

On the 10th of November, 1626, Mary left Rome with the intention of travelling to England by way of Flanders, going by way of Bavaria, where with letters from Father Domenico she would be able to meet that princely ruler Maximilian I and his wife, the Electress Elizabeth. She probably hoped also that among the more liberal minds of the German people she would find friends to speak for her in Rome when she should return to continue the struggle for the confirmation of her Institute. Besides Father Domenico's letters, she had letters from Cardinal Trescio and Father Vitelleschi,[2] whose regard for her as a person remained constant. In her party were Mary Poyntz, Elizabeth Cotton and a lay-sister—and of course the

[2] As Mary Ward intended making a short stay in Bavaria, the Father General gave her letters to members of the Society of Jesus in that region.

faithful escorts Father Henry Lee and Robert Wright. Fresh from the Roman humiliations, Mary was astonished by the princely receptions they received from the rulers in all the cities where they halted. She knew that Father Domenico's letters opened the way for her, but it must have been a solace to find that the dukes and duchesses whom she met were courteous and sympathetic as she answered their questions about her work. This was so at Florence, and again at Parma. When they arrived at Milan Mary's chief aim was to visit the Archbishop, Cardinal Borromeo, the nephew of St. Charles, to whom Mary had a lifelong devotion—the "saint of humility." As Cardinal Borromeo was a man of great austerity of life, never mixing in ordinary society nor speaking with women except in a church, Mary was advised by people who knew him not to put herself in the way of a rebuff by seeking an audience. But Mary's humility placed her beyond such reasoning, and in her quiet way she went to the Cardinal's palace to ask for an audience. In the great hall, the gentlemen-in-waiting "assured her very civilly, but for certain, that his Eminence would see no woman-kind whatever, no, not his own sister or niece—in other place than the church." While they were speaking one of the attendants left the hall and went straight to the Cardinal, telling him of the arrival of Mary and her companions. Then immediately, contrary to all precedent, the Cardinal himself came for her and led her to his private apartments, where he talked to her for more than an hour. As she took her leave, he told her that she must use his carriage while in Milan and that he would see her and her companions at the Ursuline convent before they left for Germany. He went to the convent as arranged and conversed with Mary for two hours, and then spoke with each of her companions separately, reminding them of what they owed to God for their vocation and stressing their happiness in being with Mary Ward.

As far as Lake Como they continued their journey in a coach belonging to the Cardinal; from then on for some miles it was a difficult foot-journey over the mountains in driving snow and bitter cold, across the hostile Swiss canton of the Grisons. Late on Christmas Eve they stumbled, rather than walked, into the town of Feldkirch, the first Catholic town of the Austrian Tyrol. Refreshed by a hot meal at a quiet inn, Mary and her party went out into the street again about nine o'clock to pray in the parish church until Midnight Mass, "in as great cold," writes Mary Poyntz, "as I think ever was felt."

Letters from Barbara Babthorpe in Liége had caught up with Mary at Milan, and their contents had weighed her down with sorrow. Several members in England, finding their Institute so uncertain as to its future, had returned to the world and were no credit to anyone. The same spirit had caught into its toils a section in Flanders, where there was also loss of vocations. The news, coming as it did to Mary while she was worn out with the journey, seemed to dry up her vitality, and Mary Poyntz looked at her often with a quick glance of solicitude as they knelt side by side in the cold church at Feldkirch. But Mary Ward knelt upright in deep prayer, conquering as always the pains of her weariness.

Her letters had also told her that Charles I (who had succeeded to the English throne in 1625, on the death of his father, James) was set in his Protestantism, though his intimate friends knew that at one period he had been intellectually convinced of the truth of Catholicism. His wife, Henrietta Maria of France, was a Catholic, but the Penal Laws were still in force. Brushing aside her distractions on all these matters, Mary applied herself to exercises of love, knowing that they would give more glory to God than all her anxious petitions.

At last, as midnight drew near, the sacristan walked into the sanctuary with a lighted taper and lit the candles for Mass; the church had filled with worshippers, and the joyful bells rang out over the snowy night as Mass began. A choir of Tyrolese sang the Mass in four parts. As Mary entered into the joy of the *Gloria in Excelsis* she could not wholly put away the thought of England, where there would be no singing, no bells, and, most terrible loss of all, no Mass. (*O my God, cast us not away from Thy face, and take not Thy Holy Spirit from us!*) Would it ever come right? And she bowed her head in reparation and adoration. . . .

They returned in silence to the inn after Mass, the townspeople surveying them with no little wonder. Exchange of observations at street corners and over breakfast tables only sharpened their curiosity concerning this group of foreigners who had suddenly arrived and had spent almost the whole night in the church! Curiosity was at breaking point when they saw the Ladies early next morning going by their windows towards the Capuchin church for High Mass. After Mass one matron approached to wish them a happy Christmas; then, another, with her children, paid her respects. Seeing that the tall, gentle lady was the senior, they addressed themselves to her. And all that Christmas Day Mary and her companions had to hold little receptions. As Mary Poyntz explains, referring it all to Mary's presence: "The one called the other to go and see her, each finding what suited and agreed with them, yet she always the same in equanimity, making no appearance of trying especially to please any. Her inclination would have led her to speak with no one."

We can readily understand her silence. During that second Mass, while pleading with our Infant Redeemer for the conversion of Charles I, she was given a revelation of the tenderness and long-suffering of the Divine Love towards him. The Divine Child showed "with what infinite and compassionate love He had encompassed Charles, and longed to have him for all eternity as a co-heir of His glory," but that "his own co-operation alone was wanting." In this revelation the sight of the divine love and compassion showered on Charles was such that Mary was enraptured. She confessed later to her intimate friend, Winefrid Wigmore, that had the same degree of love been manifested towards herself, she would have died of joy. Coming out to the Feldkirch streets after such divine communings, we can believe with Mary Poyntz, that "her inclination would have led her to speak with no one."

When they left Feldkirch to press on towards Munich in Bavaria, there was one more in the party. A country girl, Anna Maria Grünwaldin, spending Christmas in the town, made good use of her conversation with Mary, for by the next day she had permission to join them. She had seen how ill Mary looked, and she begged to be allowed to look after her. Added to the girl's piety was her ability to act as interpreter, as none of the Ladies spoke German. (In an age when most Catholics knew Latin, the language problem was, however, less complex than it is today.) Some years after this trip Anna Maria told a strange story. She was standing one day with Mary at a window in an inn where they stayed on the way to Bavaria. Anna, realizing that Mary was not observing the scene outside the window at all, though looking at it, asked her why she was so distracted. The following conversation took place:

Mary: "Anna Maria, what is Munich?"

Anna: "That is where the Electors of Bavaria live."

Mary: "And tell me, what is Anger?[3] Are there not nuns there, and are they not called of St. James?"

Anna: "Yes, that is so."

Mary: "Listen, Anna Maria, you and I shall go there. I shall be taken there as a false prophetess, and you will become a nun in the convent."[4]

From Feldkirch to Innsbruck: here Mary presented her credentials to the rulers, the Archduke Leopold and his wife, who had heard of her from different quarters, chiefly from the ducal rulers of Florence. The Catholic faith of the rulers of Europe in the seventeenth century gave an unworldly accent to their courtesy; they were able to look past appearances to heroism before which they abased themselves. How else account for their gracious reception and entertainment of our shabby travellers? No amount of preliminary brushing-up could hide their travel-stained appearance. It is difficult to look chic if you have been walking for nearly six weeks at the rate of fifteen miles a day; and Mary had the weary, washed-out look of a sick woman. The Archduke and his wife treated them as if they were princesses and sent them on their way in a carriage to the town of Hall,[5] where they could go by the river Inn to a river port near Munich. It was not the best weather for a sailing trip, but it carried them quickly over the last stages of their journey. They entered Munich by the gate known as the Iser Thor, a few days before the New Year of 1627.

[3] *Der Anger* ("the meadow land"), pronounced to rhyme somewhat with · our word "hanger."

[4] Both prophecies were to be fulfilled.

[5] At Hall, Mary received hospitality at a convent of Ursulines; there was mutual appreciation between this Congregation and Mary Ward.

On the previous day, while they were approaching the city over rising ground called the Iserberg, Mary was still at her meditation. When it was over she stopped her companions, and they chatted a little, though they felt a little awestruck by the supernatural atmosphere that seemed to envelop her. She looked round at their faces and asked if they would mind very much not going on to Flanders. They were surprised, but gave a murmured acquiescence to whatever she might plan. Smiling at their wondering looks, she asked: "What will you say if we obtain a house here?" Without waiting for their reply, she added: "The Elector will provide a residence for us, and will give us a yearly allowance."

13. Foundations in Bavaria, Austria and Hungary

> *"Our greatness and strength consist not in the favour of princes."*
>
> (MARY WARD)

WE ARE inclined to look on traditional stories as legends, but investigation often shows that they contain much truth. A story current in Bavaria only a few years after Mary's death explains so many things that it is probably quite accurate. Thus it runs: A few days before the New Year 1627 the Electress Elizabeth said to her husband, Maximilian: "Let us take a drive over the Iserberg; perhaps we may meet a saint." Did they take the drive? And did they notice the travel-weary pilgrims moving to the side of the road as the carriage approached? Most likely, yes. For when Mary presented herself at the palace she was immediately admitted; the ladies-in-waiting must have thought she was expected by the Electress Elizabeth and her husband. As he was the brother of Ferdinand, Prince-Bishop of Liége, he knew a great deal about Mary even before she had presented her letters. He would not hear of her continuing her journey to England, even though she said she would return to Munich. He asked, Why delay, when there was a house ready? And that is how Mary and her companions were installed in the Wein Strasse, in the mansion known as the Paradeiser Haus, which became the first house of the Institute in Bavaria. A munificent yearly allowance from Max-

imilian relieved Mary of financial worry. He covered his
generosity by remarking that it pleased him to think that, as
the English had been the first to teach his people the faith, so
now they were to teach them the manner of Christian living.[1]

As the education of girls was the special work of the Institute, steps had to be taken at once to staff and equip schools
for Maximilian. Besides being a benevolent ruler, he was well
educated, with a degree from the University of Ingoldstadt,
and he had a marked taste for the classics. He has received much
less than his due in books written by English historians, who
until recent years seemed to find much more to interest them
in the gross Hanoverians than in statesmen of Maximilian's cal-
ibre. They could make nothing of a character who, before entering on his reign, made a pilgrimage to the shrine of our Lady
at Altoetting, to whom he solemnly dedicated himself. We
need not wonder, then, at his ready appreciation of Mary
Ward, an exile from her country because of her faith. Reports
from his brother, the Prince-Bishop, about the high quality
of the education in the schools she had set up in Liége, Trèves
and Cologne, made him all the more anxious that Mary should
open a school as soon as possible in the Paradeiser Haus. He
would see to equipment. But staff! There is a letter to Barbara
Babthorpe, Provincial at Liége, from Mary, dated February
1627. It is evidently the second one on the subject of sisters
to be sent from Cologne—twelve of them—to Munich. They
came, chief among them being Winefrid Bedingfield, destined
to play an important part in the history of the Institute. She
was appointed Mistress of Schools, and was a remarkable character. When Maximilian got to know her he used to lament

[1] St. Boniface of England preached Christianity in Germany in the eighth
century.

that she was a woman, as she had qualities that would have made her an eminent statesman.

A few weeks after the school opened came a letter which the chaplain, Father Henry Lee, gave Mary to read. It was from Father Gerard in Ghent—not to Mary, of course, as he could hold no correspondence with her, being, as he was, a member of the English Province. He begins by saying how comforted he is to know that Father Lee is being so good to "God's chosen servants whom He hath tried like gold in the furnace." He wants them to know that they have the chief part of his Masses, and that he prays for them often during the day. He could get news of them if "Mother Chief Superior would write to her brother, Father George,[2] who is here with me." He wants to know all that has happened to them at Rome and Naples and is delighted that they are in Munich with Maximilian. On this subject he sends them sound advice which he intends Father Lee to pass on to Mary, that she should be chary of making any more foundations until that one is well on its feet; if it is well-established and staffed, it will make a reputation for them; and that would be better "than to strive and strain to erect others, though they were offered even by the Emperor." Father Gerard ends by saying: "I pray you tell your best friend and mine, I do of purpose forbear to write to her, but much desire to see her here, which she may very well do, her brother being here". . . . Circumstances were too strong for Mary, but we cannot but regret that she failed to follow Father Gerard's advice about opening other houses. She herself must have been a bit troubled by that sentence in his

[2] Mary Ward's youngest brother who entered the Society of Jesus a few years after leaving college in St. Omer. He would have been one of Father Gerard's "Tertians" in 1627.

letter, as she had already accepted an invitation from the Emperor Ferdinand to open a house in Vienna.

If any of the Munich community were inclined to vainglory on behalf of their Institute at the sight of princely patrons, they felt ashamed at once in Mary's presence. At her talks to them in the community room she stressed the importance of their own sanctification as their chief means of giving glory to God.

Our greatness and strength consist not in the favour of princes and great personages, but in this: that we have free and open access to God, from Whom all greatness and strength come. Let us not be content only to love Him, but let us strive to be wholly lost in His love. Do not let us be carried away by our work. We should give ourselves entirely to our Creator, and only lend ourselves to creatures. Either soon or late we shall meet troubles; it is good for us to learn early that the best way to bear them with equanimity is to thank God heartily for them. We have a strong duty to be grateful towards our benefactors; a duty also to our enemies whom we must love; we must be obliging to our companions, and courteous towards everyone. For some time to come, we shall all be very busy. Try always to show a recollected mind and do not be too careful to stand upon your rights with any who ought to yield to you; still less should you allow yourselves to dispute or quarrel with them if they oppose or contradict you. If you come in contact with the poor, be compassionate and merciful towards them, and generous, if you have the means. And, please, do not call them beggars. . . . If in your work anyone gives you trouble, meet him with friendly words; in this way you will soften both yourselves and him. Do not let us mind much what concerns us personally, but let us stand up zealously for whatever touches God and His honour. And, above all, my dear Sisters, love and speak the truth at all times.

Ferdinand II was the brother-in-law of Maximilian, who had told him at once of Mary Ward's schools for girls: boarding- and day-schools with fees, and a free school. As Maximilian had mentioned that she was a friend of Father Domenico (a special friend of the Emperor), he wrote to make doubly sure of Mary's qualities and abilities. The answer from the Carmelite father left no room for doubt, so Ferdinand wrote at once to Mary, asking her to come to Vienna. Again letters were written to the houses for a staff, and some time in August the schools in Vienna were opened. The Emperor's offer to Mary was one that many Reverend Mothers must dream of sometimes: she was to choose any house in the city that pleased her, and he would arrange for schools nearby! She chose a new house in which *eighteen* families lived; they left amicably with a generous compensation. Spacious schools and a yearly revenue from the imperial coffers—what a dream! Among the boarders were girls from the best families in Vienna. In the three schools there were about five hundred girls before Christmas.

Mary Ward would willingly have consolidated her work in Munich and Vienna, but another pressing invitation came to her, this time from Hungary, just as she had opened the schools in Vienna. In Hungary, Cardinal Pazmanny was confronted in the city of Pressburg by a strong Calvinist drive—there were in that city as many Calvinists as Catholics. The Cardinal clearly saw that the education of the girls, who would be the wives and mothers of the next generation, would do more to reclaim the population than the most stringent imperial edicts against heresy. When the situation was thus put before Mary, her zeal threw caution to the winds, and she accepted the Cardinal's invitation. Did she not feel also that the more widely her work was known among ecclesiastics, the nearer would be the realization of her heart's desire: the confirmation of her Institute in Rome? All these foundations were in her mind a necessary stage in the foundation of a Religious Institute for the conversion of England. So, again a breaking of new ground; and the girls in Pressburg were the gainers, as they flocked to the schools where Barbara Babthorpe was the Superior.

The country known to us as Czechoslovakia was, in the seventeenth century, Bohemia; Prague was the capital. Until the recent Communist domination of the country, the Institute of the Blessed Virgin Mary was doing a magnificent work of education which had its origins in Mary Ward's acceptance of an invitation from a Catholic nobleman, a friend of the Emperor, to establish a house in Prague.[3] Let us observe that all these invitations, *and their acceptance*, were in the one year (1627) and that the Munich foundation was not a year old. Caught up in such activity, we might expect Mary to be confused, but she seems to have moved from one event to the other with a gentleness that no worldly commerce could shatter. Her early biographer testifies to this by saying that "in almost every occurrence, whether pleasurable or painful, she was drawn without any self-seeking to contemplate God only, and to have no wish for anything but what He willed and because He willed it. And this was not sleepily and by the way, but with full desire and peace of soul, so that she confessed with much simplicity, that she could find no true satisfaction in any other thing, but in the most holy will of God."

Mary had need of all her fortitude in the months—and in-

[3] The house was not founded in Mary's lifetime.

deed, the years—that now opened before her. The first intimation that her season of prosperity was over came to her in Prague, where the Archbishop, Cardinal Harrach, took up an attitude of opposition that grew in intensity as he found that the Emperor was throwing his weight into the scale on behalf of the English Ladies. The Apostolic Nuncio in Prague supported the Cardinal, who was influenced in the matter by a Capuchin friar, Father Valerio de'Magni, lately come from Rome and Provincial of his order in the northern countries. His sermons against Mary and her companions contained the old, familiar charges, emanating from the agents of the English Clergy in Rome. When Father Valerio turned the Cardinal in Prague against Mary, he thought he was doing a service to God. (Ironically enough, he was later imprisoned for heresy, in a field quite apart from this one of mistaken zeal.) In Vienna, Cardinal Klessel, hearing Father Valerio's charges, and being anxious to exercise episcopal jurisdiction over the house of the English Ladies, began to have second thoughts about their zeal and wrote his doubts to the Pope. Mary may have heard of this letter; she did *not* know that while she was waiting in Prague at Easter, 1628, for the situation to become more favourable in that town, Pope Urban in Rome had actually summoned at the Vatican a private congregation composed of four cardinals, to decide what measures should be taken to break up the houses of the English Ladies in the various countries. It was decided by the Pope and cardinals to act through the legates in these countries, thus preventing the necessity for issuing a papal bull. For this purpose, the Apostolic Nuncio at Vienna was to confer with the Emperor and Empress; and the legate at Brussels was to proceed in like manner with the Archduchess Isabella concerning Flanders. It seems certain that Mary was unaware of the gravity of the situation, though her heart sank as one rumour after another fluttered from Rome over the Alps.

A controversy more immediately at hand in Munich was occupying most of her attention. It had called her from Prague. The trouble on this occasion had its roots in the enthusiastic approval of a bishop—the Bishop of Bayreuth—who, while visiting Munich, so admired the system of education in Mary Ward's schools that he asked her to take over the houses of some Ursulines in his diocese *with the Ursulines in them*. Not even the youngest Ursuline postulant was to be allowed a protesting squeak. The lives of three hundred women were to be rearranged—all Germans, who may have felt no taste at all for the conversion of England. (The youngest postulant probably had to examine a map to find out its location.) Behind their submissive acquiescence to the Bishop, there must have been some despairing hearts. The Bishop sought to make his ukase less distasteful by assuring them that he would see that they did not have to go through another novitiate, but would be professed at once in their new home with the English Ladies. Even the Bishop's confessor and the Ursulines' confessor urged the plan, though they were Religious priests and should have seen how preposterous the whole idea was. (Make no mistake: the seventeenth century was a *man's* world.) Mary Ward gently but firmly refused to have anything to do with it. The Bishop and the priests were deeply annoyed, and so far forgot their charity as to tell Mary that they would deprive her and her Institute of every friend they had in Bavaria and Austria. As the Bishop and those connected with him stood well at every court, the threat was no merely verbal one. Maximilian was the first to be approached, but his friendship for the English Ladies was too strong thus to be broken, and he approved of what Mary had done. But she was wise in making up her mind to go to Rome to find out just how well or how badly stood the affairs of the Institute in papal circles.

14. Suppression of the Institute

"In detachment the spirit finds quiet and repose."

(ST. JOHN OF THE CROSS)

MARY'S HEALTH, which had been deteriorating for some years, gave cause for great anxiety in the community of the Paradeiser Haus in Munich during the Christmas season of 1628. The internal organic trouble which had declared itself while she was at Perugia in 1624 flared up anew when her physical resistance was worn down by the trying events of 1628. She was in such pain that no posture gave her relief. (In our century she would have been taken to a hospital, operated on, and made comfortable.) The Munich doctor who attended her did what he could; but when she announced, in the temporary comfort after a spasm of pain, that she was going to Rome, he must have wondered if there was a mental symptom that had escaped his diagnosis. "Go to Rome? You will die before you pass the Iser Thor!" And he said a spate of other things in good German, as would any other doctor confronted by a very sick patient intent on a suicidal journey. He used his authority to the extent of saying that she was to go in a litter (the seventeenth-century version of an ambulance, carried by bearers on foot). So, in the early days of the New Year, 1629, the party set out in a snowstorm, the bearers probably thinking they had been hired by a party of madmen. Father Henry Lee and Robert Wright were there of course, and sweetened the

128

tempers of the bearers. Winefrid Wigmore, Elizabeth Cotton and a faithful lay-sister, Anne Turner, were Mary's companions. (Winefrid had been summoned to Munich from Naples during the Prague worry.) It was a dreadful journey for all, Mary hanging on to life by a thread most of the way. Her digestion was in such a state that she could eat nothing but a little water-gruel, given several times a day; and her stomach rejected even that, half an hour after taking. "They asked her once [Winefrid writes] 'if she thought she should reach Rome alive.' She replied, 'that there was more appearance she should not, than that she should, neither did it import her where she died, in her bed or under a hedge, so it were in her fidelity to God.' That 'she had made several general confessions, and lately one for her last, her daily Communions had been for many years for her last; for the rest she was sure, lived she or died she, she served a good Master.' "

On arriving in Rome they went straight to the house they had bought in 1622 and still owned; and in no time clever Anne Turner had a bed made up, and was giving an extra pat to the pillows to let Mother Mary Ward know how well she was going to look after her. Three weeks the patient lay there, mending slowly, but surely, now that she was in the same city as the Holy Father. Winefrid Wigmore felt dismayed when she reviewed the situation. They were no better off in the way of having an advocate than when they left Rome in 1626; their chief idea in going to the Elector Maximilian of Bavaria at that time was to enlist his sympathy, so that when they returned to Rome, they might have letters from him to the Pope. Were they wise in returning to Rome to fight their battle alone? At this stage Winefrid would pull herself up short. Why all this pessimism? No one, surely, could believe the nonsense Mary's enemies were saying against her—that she preached in the streets and only failed to mount the pulpit in churches because the priests would not allow such arrogance? . . . It was hinted that other charges, of a scurrilous nature, were made. . . . But Winefrid drove the whole thing from her mind and showed a cheerful countenance to Mary, whom she encouraged in her idea of drawing up a memorial to present to Pope Urban when she was well enough to have an audience with him. They both decided to omit all mention of the personal charges. Why waste time over such disagreeable stuff?

At the end of three weeks Mary was strong enough to go to the Vatican for her audience. Winefrid went with her, and they both enjoyed the warmth of the early spring morning as they crossed the squares where the fountains rippled and tossed their spray in musical cadences which have been the song of Rome for centuries, even in the days of Horace, who wrote of "the splash of fountains with jets of water clear."

In the audience chamber in the Vatican, Pope Urban received Mary with his usual kindness. He was sorry she was not well; and did Princess Constanza know she was in Rome? . . . What did Urban think about Mary as he made her sit by him and received the parchment memorial which she gave him? He looked sad as he opened it and mentally reviewed the situation. Did she not know that her case was hopeless? That nearly a year ago the Nuncios in the various countries had received papal orders to suppress the houses of the Institute? It was quite clear that none of those Nuncios wanted to do the unpleasant job. And there was the Prince-Bishop of Liége writing to say he didn't quite understand what was required of him. Would the Pope please give further instructions? The same kind of letter came from the Nuncio in Brussels. It was clear they were all hedging for time. The Pope felt glad that Mary had so many good friends. Perhaps this visit of hers to Rome would mean that the suppression need never take place. She might modify her plans. As they stood, they were far too revolutionary for the Cardinals, and for his Holiness also. . . . And here was their saintly author saying to him in her gentle voice: "Never shall I oppose myself to the wishes of your Holiness; even if it meant that the toil of years should go for nothing."

After glancing through the memorial with her and listening as she stressed several of the points, his Holiness stood, and with princely Barberini courtesy helped Mary to rise. He had given her his instructions: that she should make a précis of the memorial and he would appoint two impartial scrutineers to study it. Cardinal Mellino (who had been the chief mover in the closing of the schools in 1625) and the Father General of the Jesuits were the two appointed. At hearing their names Mary said: "Neither is friendly." The Pope looked surprised and said that he knew the Father General was very well disposed to her. She shook her head. But the Pope reiterated that Father Vitelleschi *was* friendly. And Mary let the subject drop.

Back in her room she discussed the audience with Winefrid, who had waited for her outside the audience chamber. "Not Father Vitelleschi!" was Winefrid's dismayed exclamation. The report made by him and Cardinal Mellino was of no help at all; and the Pope, still anxious to save Mary's work, appointed another congregation of four cardinals, before whom Mary herself was to appear, declaring what she desired and her reasons. The leader of the four cardinals was Cardinal Borgia, grand-nephew of St. Francis Borgia. All four were fine characters, keenly aware of their responsibility in being entrusted with the decision on a subject which had become a major anxiety in Vatican circles. Mary Ward prepared for the meeting, sustained only by the confidence that her life was enclosed in the divine will, and that the fatherly providence of God would care for her. A racking cough made Winefrid look at her often as she sat by the window resting a little before they set out for the Vatican. She would have to speak, and how could she, with that cough? . . . Soon they were on the way . . . and Mary was being led into the conference chamber.

Mary spoke for forty-five minutes, in a clear voice without any trace of a cough, while the cardinals followed her intently, Cardinal Borgia's dark eyes in his fine Spanish face showing the reverence he felt for this heroic Englishwoman. She gave a sketch of the Institute, its origin and work, and the esteem in which it was held by Catholic sovereigns in Flanders, Bavaria and Austria. There was nothing either apologetic or belligerent about her statements; she merely stated facts, and courteously remarked at one stage that she understood and reverenced the vigilance of the cardinals in examining closely such a new project as her proposed Institute. If his Holiness and their Eminences thought it good that she should desist, she should at once humbly submit to their decision. She and her companions were in no haste; what was not done in one year could be done in another. She would gladly wait for God's time, for we had to follow, not go before, Him. At the end of three-quarters of an hour Mary folded her notes and rested her hands on the table before her. The cardinals murmured their satisfaction, and she and they withdrew by different doors. Thus ended an incident that must be without its peer in Vatican history.

So impressed was Cardinal Borgia that he sought out the Pope at once to relate all that had happened. Then, in a grave voice, he said that he believed Mary's project was divinely inspired, and that he could not in conscience work against it. On the other hand he felt powerless to assist her, so many and so powerful were her enemies. He ended by saying: "I humbly entreat your Holiness that I may be excused from dealing any further in the matter." The Pope yielded to his entreaty, and sighed to see how little he himself seemed able to do for Mary. If she would only modify some of her demands; for instance, that idea that the Institute should be subject to a Mother General, rather than to any bishop. That in itself was enough to make enemies for her among the clergy. But Mary clung to her idea, extravagant as it seemed to the Papacy of 1629. On this point her wisdom was not vindicated until 1703, and then it was by another Pope, Clement XI, in the epoch-making decree: *Lasciate governare le donne dalle donne* ("Let women be governed by women").

After the meeting with the cardinals, Mary seems to have made no attempt to see the Pope again, contenting herself by leaving an explanation for him with Princess Constanza, whom she saw frequently. The Princess was deeply concerned about Mary's health, but she refrained from questioning her friend on her meeting with the cardinals; refrained, too, from telling her that she and her Institute were discussed with much sympathy in aristocratic circles. Then, since the Princess (papal relationship notwithstanding) liked to sift the news that came her way, she asked Mary whether there was any truth in the report that Cardinal Bandino had offered what he and many others thought was an admirable solution of the deadlock:

"That if you would accept the modified enclosure observed at the Torre dei Specchi, you would be allowed to set up as many houses, all over the world, as you liked."

This tempting offer had in fact been made, and Mary had rejected it. But how could she explain this in a way to make the Princess understand what had baffled the cardinals? For her special apostolate, unity under a single head was essential, but even more essential in England and the other Protestant countries was freedom of movement. She "would not," said Mary, "admit two sticks put in a cross in form of enclosure." How hard to make this clear at a time and in a city where not nuns alone but well-bred ladies would never be seen in the streets.

Whether or not Mary's friend finally understood her reasons for refusing to modify any part of what, Mary believed, had come to her by divine inspiration, she still held her in most tender affection. As she left, she whispered to Mary: "If ever I can do anything for you, my dear, dear friend, call on me at once."

There was one other close friend who was following (from Father Henry Lee's reports) Mary Ward's affairs: that was Father Gerard, who was stationed in Rome, where he was confessor to the English College. We do not hear that he met Mary during this visit; but letters from him to the Munich house, written a few months after this visit of Mary's, show that he was following with grieved intentness the disastrous curve of the Institute's descent into the valley of humiliation.

Mary, back with her community in Vienna, showed them the beautiful silks she had bought at Venice on the foot-journey home from Rome. She had spent money thus on altar furnishings and vestments, though the price of a pair of shoes was evidently beyond her means. The Munich community had some remarks to make on this matter to Winefrid Wigmore after they had seen their Reverend Mother limping in the doorway at the end of the journey. Investigations showed that she had made the journey in ill-fitting shoes, someone's cast-offs.[1] Winefrid had to undergo some pertinent sisterly cross-examinations: Why didn't she see that Mother had a decent pair of shoes? Couldn't Winefrid have put aside some money for that necessity? Winefrid bore it all, not silently, but with a few defensive sallies. Then, with mock condescension: "Listen, my poor children, have you ever tried to talk finance with Mother on the bread-and-butter level? No, you have not. Now, how would you begin to talk about a comfortable pair of shoes to a saint who wants to buy silk for the altar? When I told her on leaving Rome that we had scarcely enough money for the journey, she laughed and said: 'I have found out a good way to make our monies hold out—to be sure to deny no poor body an alms who shall ask it on the road' . . . Now, you go and argue, yourselves, with Mother about shoes. . . . "

Mary chose Vienna rather than Munich in which to await some communication from Rome as a result of her exposition before the four cardinals. She knew that a reply would come by the usual diplomatic channel, a message to the Apostolic Nuncio. There was no Nuncio in Munich, but one in Vienna at the Austrian court. Winefrid Wigmore she sent to Liége to represent her, and to quiet turbulent elements in the community. Mary Poyntz remained Superior at Munich. Mary had been with her community in Vienna less than a month when news arrived from Naples that the Archbishop of that city

---

[1] The shoes are kept among relics at the Institute in Altoetting, Bavaria.

had carried out the decree of dissolution sent out in July 1628. Mary felt ill as she read the report. It was some comfort to read also that the decree had produced a wave of discontent throughout Naples. The gentlemen of the city united in sending a memorial to the Pope's brother, Cardinal Barberini, deprecating the loss of "the heroic and holy labours of the English Ladies, by whom the daughters of the place have been educated in all suitable arts and in virtue." Further, the Cardinal was asked to use his influence to restore the community and their schools, as there were no other helps for their daughters in Naples. This memorial is dated September 6, 1629. The first blows of suppression had fallen on the Institute, which disappeared forever from Naples. Yet in Vienna work went on as usual. Surely something would happen before the decree was carried out in Bavaria and Austria. In Munich ten lovely English girls arrived at the novitiate and were received. Among them were two Babthorpes, nieces of Barbara; a niece of Winefrid Wigmore, and Frances Bedingfield,[2] sister of Winefrid Bedingfield.

A letter to Mary Poyntz from Father Gerard, dated October 6, 1629, from Rome, shows more clearly than any explanations of ours the presence of a crisis in Institute affairs. It is a long letter—really a pamphlet—and was clearly meant to be read by as many of the religious as possible. He was moved to write it by reports current in Rome of the disloyalty of some Superiors and senior members in Flanders, chiefly in Liége. The reports were only too true, for there was a movement on foot in Flanders to repudiate Mary Ward as foundress; the

---

[2] Foundress of the Bar Convent, Institute of the Blessed Virgin Mary, York.

members concerned hoped thus to avert the suppression of the Institute, which they saw was imminent. Among the disloyal religious was Elizabeth Ward, Mary's sister, who left the Institute. We need not discourse on the sorrowful theme; it was more than a drop in Mary's bitter chalice.

To return to Father Gerard's letter: he begins by assuring Mary Poyntz (and, through her, the whole Institute) of his unchangeable affection and esteem for them, "no matter what storm, tempests or disturbances may be raised against you at home or abroad." He passes on to his main theme: the harm that the disloyal religious are doing to the very existence of the Institute, in Vatican circles where the idea grows apace that it should be suppressed at once if the members cannot remain loyal to their foundress. The enemies of the Institute were bringing that point to the fore in all their discussions. Father Gerard is clearly distressed about it and begs all the members to remain loyal to Mary Ward:

. . . The purer you preserve the spirit of your venerable Mother, and the closer you keep to her footsteps, the nearer you will be to God, and thus united you will be a terror to your enemies. It may be that the wicked enemy by the permission of God will for a while impede your labours; but fully to destroy what God through His servant has begun is impossible except you yourselves will it. . . . It is no little blessing that God has given you, to call you to this vocation in the lifetime of your Mother and Foundress, at having lived with her, conversed with her, experienced her manner of governing, having heard her counsels, and been a witness to her exemplary and toilsome life. . . . Engrave all her words, works and maxims in your hearts; for the time will come when you will desire them, but shall not have them. You will always have enemies, and you will never be in want of contradictions either in or out of the house, but you will not have her always with you. She is now no longer young, neither is she healthy, but always ailing, no longer strong, but very weak, and in a word not living but always in a dying state. Make use then of the short time God will still leave her with you. . . . For she has not only been sent amongst you to give you rules but also to teach you how to follow them. . . .

One of Mary's chief enemies was almost at her door in Munich. He was Father Adam Contzen, S.J., Rector of the Jesuit house in Munich. Yet he had once been friendly. Was he included in those to whom Father Gerard referred in veiled language in his letter: "Some who formerly praised everything, now blame everything; those who before consoled all now oppress them; those who formerly approved of all now abuse all . . ."? Most likely he was, for the defection on the part of his own brethren was a cause of keen distress to Father Gerard, whose own nature was so steadfast.

At intervals rumours percolated from Rome to Vienna that it would be only a matter of months before the Institute was formally suppressed. Yet Mary Ward radiated peace, praying and waiting; her community could only try to follow where she led along the way of abandonment to divine providence. Then, one day came the shattering rumour that Mary herself was to be imprisoned as a heretic. Mary had a steady premonition that this was no mere rumour, but her serenity was unaltered: "Everything comes to us as a grace when we love God. We have been called to a vocation of love; and no matter where we are put, we can go on loving God and giving glory to Him. We have only one thing to fear: to fear that we may be afraid; and even that fear we need not have when we are ready to suffer much with Our Lord." But the thought of the ignominy that was to come on their revered foundress and Mother was almost too much for the faith of some of the community. One evening as a few of them sat at recreation with Mary, she led them sweetly to face the dread idea of her imprisonment; but a young nun, her voice husky with unshed tears, broke out: "I could almost take it unkindly at the hand of Almighty God—" Mary turned a severe face towards her to say: "If you thought so, it would be impossible to love you; beware not to let such a thought come into your mind." The young nun bent her head over her sewing, blinking to keep back her tears. (The hemming on her cuff that evening was not worth much.) When the bell rang for dormitory duty, she rose and went for Mary's blessing, giving her an embarrassed little smile as she knelt. The firm pressure of the hand in blessing rested for an extra second, speaking forgiveness, encouragement, affection.

At the end of 1630 Mary left Vienna for Munich. It was now only a matter of waiting. In January 1631 the blow fell. On January 13 Pope Urban signed the Bull of Suppression of the Institute. Mary was ill in bed at the time; she received the news quietly. After spending some time in prayer, she felt sure that her imprisonment was also at hand. She said to Mary Poyntz: "I hinder my friends from their design; I will go abroad that they may see I am not afraid, nor unwilling they do their pleasure." So she got up and went into the city, and that chapter of the chronicle ends thus: "Her plan had its effect, for on the 7th of February (then a Friday), about four of the clock in the afternoon, came to our house the Dean of

Our Blessed Lady her church[3] in Munich with two canons of the same church, and produced a letter addressed to himself, which he read in this tenor: 'Take Mary Ward as a heretic, schismatic, and rebel to the Holy Church.' "

[3] In modern English: Our Lady's church.

15. The Imprisonment of Mary Ward

"Je schmachvoller desto lieber."[1]
(MARY WARD TO THE GERMAN DEAN)

ON THE day that the Dean and the canons called at the Paradeiser Haus with the warrant for Mary's imprisonment she was too ill to go downstairs to receive them, so they came to her room where she was sitting. She received them cheerfully; but when the Dean pronounced the word "heretic" she shuddered, although she allowed herself no gesture but a reverent sign of the cross. Mary Poyntz and Elizabeth Cotton were in the room, the two canons in the doorway—and these two young priests openly wiped away the tears which they could not restrain. The Dean faltered as he further read a clause about summoning the secular arm of the law if it was needed. "Oh no," said Mary gently, "I would not give you that trouble; it would not be fitting for me to make any resistance. I shall go to whatever prison you like. The more ignominious the better. Suffering without sin is no burden." When the Dean suggested that they wait for nightfall before going to the Anger convent where she was to be imprisoned, Mary lifted her head slightly to say with dignity: "By no means. The more it is known the better. Why should I seek the darkness when I am innocent? I have always loved the light, and have no need now to hide my actions." (By this time Elizabeth had gone and returned with

[1] "The more humiliating the dearer." (This literal translation has more force than the usual English rendering.)

141

Anne Turner, who began quietly putting Mary's things together.)

After conversing for some time in a cheerful manner with the Dean, Mary rose to go, saying as she stood: "May I say good-bye to the sisters, your Lordship?" The Dean uncomfortably said he could not allow that. To break up the miserable group Mary made us if to go, saying that she would be able to walk to the Anger. But the Dean, relieved, and glad to be making some contribution to her comfort, said a carriage was waiting at the door. Mary asked for a minute or so to pray: "She knelt down for the space of a *Pater* and an *Ave* in the same room and then prepared silently to leave the house."

Because of Mary Ward's poor health, the lay-sister, Anne Turner, was allowed to accompany her and to stay with her at the Poor Clares' Convent at the Anger. These Franciscan sisters had been startled to receive notice from the Dean that they were to guard a heretic woman who was to be entrusted to their vigilance. When Mary and Anne Turner stepped from the carriage at the door of the convent they saw a small group of nuns and some Franciscan priests waiting to receive them. One of the Franciscans was the Commissary of his order. The waiting group expected to have difficulty in managing the "monstrous heretic" who was to be imprisoned in a cell in the convent. When Mary approached them with her calm, dignified demeanour, their dread turned to reverence. One holy sister saw through the human mistake so clearly that she hastened to pray in the chapel. Later she sought out her abbess to say: "My Mother, how are we misinformed. This is a great servant of God, whom we have received, and our house is happy in her setting foot in it. Let me have at least the happiness of going to look at her at the door, although I am not permitted to speak to her." By the next day, the whole Poor Clare community was of the same opinion.

But in this house cleanliness was a long way after godliness. The room into which Mary and Anne Turner were locked was dirty and evil-smelling A nun dying from consumption had lately occupied it. "She hath spit up all her lungs," wrote Mary graphically. Anne Turner doubted if any of these Poor Clares had been trained in a novitiate; certainly not in one of Mother Mary Ward's, where the novices had to learn by heart the rules, one of which (how pertinent it seemed now!) was: "Cleanliness, as being conducive both to health and edification, must be the concern of all, both as to themselves and all things beside. . . . " Mary herself thought of the clean rooms in the convent of the Poor Clares in Flanders. To her as to us this dirty room was a mystery—but what a nauseating reality! As Anne Turner grunted and slapped the pillows about, trying to find the cleanest spot for Mary's head, her Superior tried to cheer her up by saying that perhaps there was a nice view from the window. With a soiled sheet in her hand Anne went to the high window, which was partly nailed up with boards; perched on a chair to look out the dormer window, she turned on Mary a look of horror: "It's a cemetery, Mother!" . . . Part of the sentence of imprisonment was that Mary should send any letters she had to send through the Dean or the Abbess. She had some communications to make that were for her nuns alone. Lemon-juice was the first thing necessary (writing in it being invisible until the paper is heated).

As she composed herself for sleep on her uncomfortable bed, she put her whole life once again into the hands of God: "Father, into Thy hands I commend my spirit." She felt her life was over, and in great peace she accepted death in whatever form God should arrange for her. She put it all into His hands; she could do nothing more to put things right. She would try to suffer with Our Lord in the time that remained—it would not be long: "Show me, O Lord, Thy mercy: and grant me Thy salvation." . . . But sleep would not come. What was that fluttering thought that she drove away as soon as it emerged into her consciousness? She was not to lie down and die? She was to work and vindicate her innocence! She fought against the thought for a time; then, feeling that perhaps it had a heavenly sender, she agreed and resolved to do all she could in that regard. Almost immediately sleep came and stayed till morning.

Next day at the Paradeiser Haus, the school routine went on as usual, though the children must have wondered why their mistresses looked different—some paler, some with dark rings about their eyes. With great self-control the nuns moved from one class to the other, though the thoughts of all were with that loved prisoner whom perhaps they would never see again. Except for those we have mentioned, none of the forty nuns in the house had known what had happened until their Superior (Mary Poyntz) told them in the community room, whither they had been summoned after the carriage had driven away. When the dreadful news was announced, the general murmur of horrified distress was almost more than the Superior could bear. She guessed, rather than knew, how Mary Ward had wept over each one of them at night during the last few months, wondering what would become of them when the suppression took place. Mary Poyntz felt helpless before their unspoken anguish and was relieved when it was time to go to the chapel. She asked them to remember that Mother Mary Ward was particularly anxious that they should not murmur resentfully among themselves over what was happening but should try to take it peacefully as their portion in the Passion of Our Lord.

As Mary Poyntz sat at her desk writing letters to the pupils' mothers[2] the next day, she thought of the previous afternoon, when every gesture and look of her dear friend and spiritual mother had gone to her heart. Before Mary Ward had entered the carriage she gave the Dean a message for the Elector Maximilian—a message to thank him for his thought of her in keeping from her the knowledge of this development. There was no sarcasm in her message; she was so accustomed to giving everyone's actions the best interpretation possible that she would not allow into her mind the bitter thought that Maximilian and his wife had failed her. But Mary Poyntz caught a glimpse of disappointment in the low voice which said for her alone: "Let us not mind; mortification and suffering are best for us when most complete." Then she had stepped into the carriage. *O my God!* was the silent cry of Mary Poyntz as she put down her pen. . . . A knock at the door. "Come in." "Mother, there are two Franciscan Fathers in the guest room —to see you." "Very well, thank you, Sister." Mary Poyntz waited for the door to close after the sister, then rested her head on her hands. *Franciscans. . . . What do they want? O my God, give me the gift of a perfect faith! . . . to see you in every priest. . . . Yet I feel that I cannot bear the sight of any priest's habit unless he is ministering the sacraments. . . . Dear Lord, teach me to love my enemies.*

Then she rose and went downstairs, fortifying herself by the thought of Mary Ward's charity. She received the Franciscan Fathers with gentle courtesy and soon realized that they

2 The parents were asked to remove their pupils as soon as possible.

had come in kindness to give a report on Mary Ward, whose cheerfulness and courage had so impressed them that they were convinced of her innocence. If Mother Superior would like to make her more comfortable, she could send a mattress and bed-clothes to the Anger convent; further, if the sisters wished to send the special dishes of food which Mother Mary Ward's delicate health needed, they would be given to her. . . . As the priests took their leave, Mary Poyntz made a mental note in favour of Franciscans.

The papers that came round the food were sent back to Mary Poyntz and the others—carefully folded papers for the next food parcel, each bearing letters written in invisible lemon juice, pathetic and affectionate little messages back and forth. "We can only," wrote Mary, "read once a day what you write, wanting fire . . . sometimes we fry, and sometimes we freeze." The real and pressing object of Mary's communications was to give instructions to Mary Poyntz concerning the memorials that must be sent to Rome, for they were both convinced—and rightly so—that the Pope knew nothing of the imprisonment. To let him know what had happened was Mary Ward's solemn resolution on that first night at the Anger. In spite of her dire bodily weakness her mind must have remained very clear, for on the third day of her imprisonment she had drawn up two memorials, one for the Pope, the other for the Cardinals in Rome. To communicate with them was the one thing her enemies sought to prevent; they knew not the potency of lemon juice, never having known what persecution was until they took a hand at it themselves.

Both memorials were to go from the community at the Paradeiser Haus, stating that they were "by all those of whatsoever nation that live under the government of Mother Maria

Ward." The one to the Cardinals stressed the horror they felt that their revered foundress should be imprisoned on a charge of heresy. To put her in prison in her present state amounted to putting her to death. The memorial to the Pope told all that had happened concerning Mary's imprisonment and concluded by stressing the state of Mary's health: "Vouchsafe, then, to call her to Rome. Give her leave at least once to speak in her own cause, the case being made so public, and that of which she is accused, and for which she is thus treated, so enormous." The documents once sent to Rome, strain was lifted from the community at the Paradeiser Haus, for they felt that the right machinery had been set in motion. That did not prevent them from asking guardian angels every day to take the letters to and fro under their very special angelic protection; the community had learnt that devotion from their foundress. So, humourous little bits of house news are told in lemon juice, and they gather round the community-room fire every evening to hold to the heat the scraps of paper with the lemon-juice writing that was their share of the notes. They found it quite natural that their Superior should have private ones for herself and Mother Elizabeth Cotton. But no amount of cheerful conspiring could take away the terrible fact that Mary Ward was allowed neither Mass nor the sacraments. They turned to their Superior: "Mother, if the Dean is frightened of the Inquisition, surely the Elector Maximilian is not." Maximilian *was* frightened of opposing the long arm of the Inquisition, but by dint of asking, Mary Poyntz at last obtained for Mary Ward the privilege of going to Mass. Confession and Holy Communion were still withheld.

The close confinement and unwholesome atmosphere of her prison room were the worst things in the world for Mary's health. She began to feel as though she were dying; and she *was* dying. The incoming notes begged her to ask for a doctor; and she replied by asking them to go to see the Electress Elizabeth with the request that she send her own physician to see the prisoner. The Electress granted the request at once, and Anne Turner tried to furbish the ugly, evil-smelling room to prepare for his visit. The court physician wrinkled his nose somewhat on entering. Without even examining Mary he said bluntly that she would die if she were left in that nauseating atmosphere; he himself lingered not on the threshold, but, knowing his duty, he came for other visits. Meanwhile the Paradeiser nuns were appealing for a change in the place of her imprisonment; but in vain; the Elector said it was beyond his jurisdiction. Mary's fever increased, and on the ninth day after the physician's first visit he said she must receive the Last Sacraments, as she was actually dying. When the Dean was asked permission for the Last Sacraments, he said she would have to abjure her heresy. (Could obscurantism go further?) The poor Dean drew up the paper and sent it to Mary to sign. She took the paper and saw there the words, that "if she had ever said or done anything contrary to Faith or Holy Church, she repented. . . ." In a low voice she asked the Abbess if "his Holiness or the Holy Office required such a thing." When she heard that it was merely the Dean's idea, she said with great firmness and serenity: "God forbid that I, to cancel venial sins which, through God's mercies, are all I have to accuse myself of, should commit a mortal sin, and cast so great a blot upon so many innocent and deserving persons, by saying 'If I have done or said anything against Holy Church.' My '*If*,' with what is already acted by my adversaries, would give just cause to the world to believe I suffer justly. No, no. I will cast myself rather on the mercy of Jesus Christ and die without the sacraments." She sank back on her pillow and closed her eyes with exhaustion. Then raising herself on her arm, and with a tranquil face, she asked for paper and ink. Anne Turner was now alone with her and supported her while she wrote, resting for a few minutes every now and again:

I have never done or said anything, either great or small, against his Holiness (whose holy will I have offered myself, and do now offer myself, wholly to obey), or the authority of Holy Church. But on the contrary, my feeble powers and labours have been for twenty-six years, entirely, and as far as was possible to me, employed for the honour and service of both, as I hope, by the mercy of God, and the benignity of his Holiness, will be manifested in due time and place. Nor would I now for a thousand worlds . . . do the least thing unfitting the dutiful service of a true Catholic and a most obedient of Holy Church. Nevertheless, if that, which was at the first allowed and authorized by the Supreme Pontiffs, or Sacred Congregations of Cardinals, in which according to my poor capacity I have desired and sought to serve Holy Church . . . should be repugnant to the duty of a true Christian . . . I am . . . most ready to acknowledge my fault, to ask pardon for the offence, and, together with the public dishonour already laid on me, to offer my poor and brief life in satisfaction of the said sin.

After several pauses to gather her failing strength, Mary at last finished and signed it, putting the date and place: Munich, March 27, 1631. The Abbess delivered it to the Dean with a note from Mary explaining that she could sign no other paper, and that the responsibility now lay with him of her dying without the sacraments. The Dean gave leave at once, and Mary enclosed herself in the sanctuary of her own soul to prepare for the sacrament of Extreme Unction.

The convent confessor, a Franciscan priest, administered the sacrament while the Abbess and nuns of the Anger stood reverently around her bed. Most of them were crying softly; even the priest could not restrain his tears. Mary had no tears; her face showed the peace that possessed her soul. At the end of a short thanksgiving she opened her eyes and made signs to Anne that she wished to rise and be dressed. The priest had gone, but the nuns had lingered; and now they all thought Mary must be delirious. But she sat up and said in a clear voice: "Nay, I am myself; I know what I do; I must take leave of my dear Sisters, Mother Abbess will not deny me the grace to see and speak with them at the grille. And you," turning to the nuns, "will have the charity to carry me into the church." No one but Mary knew that she had sent word to Mary Poyntz to be there with some of the community at this precise hour. The nuns carried her to the church and left her alone with Anne Turner by the grille. Their foundress told her community to take courage and to put all their confidence in God, who would not let her die unless it were most for His glory. Then, summoning all her strength, she said: "Whatever happens you must have no bitterness against the people who have made us suffer. You must forgive them cordially and entirely and pray for them heartily."

When the Poor Clares carried Mary up to her cell, they thought she would die in their arms. They put her to bed and she lapsed into unconsciousness, lying thus through the afternoon and evening. About nine o'clock she fell into a natural sleep, out of which she woke refreshed. As Anne bent towards her (dear Anne Turner, you always seemed to be watching from your straw pallet on the floor) Mary said: "I know not what Our Lord wills to do with me; but it seems to me I am better." . . . Later in the morning the doctor called, expecting to find her dead; he blinked to see her sitting up in bed, looking wan, no doubt, but healthy and cheerful. After making sure that he himself was quite normal, he hurried off to tell the Electress Elizabeth the good news. He said that "in Mary's condition it was a miracle to be recovering in whatever place; but that to recover in that room, which was sufficient alone to have killed her, had she been in her best health, was a manifest interposition of God, in order to make her innocence clear before all men."

Mary's own grateful note to the community in the Paradeiser Haus told them of her renewed health. (They could hardly believe her news, being still shaken by the sorrowful leave-taking at the grille on the previous day.) She wrote as she had written so often: "All will pass." Then she praised the great charity of the Poor Clares. Not a word of censure for anyone, just a humorous little ending: "Sure my soul and body gain by this bargain." Still the Paradeiser nuns waited anxiously for an answer to the memorials they had sent to Rome.

At last a letter came direct to them from the Pope; it contained a mandate ordering Mary's immediate release. Only later did it come out that on receiving the memorials the Pope had called a particular congregation of cardinals, at which he presided in person, and caused the whole affair to be discussed before him. When he heard how all had passed, he expressed himself as much displeased by Mary's imprisonment, and ordered a decree to be prepared setting her at liberty. . . . When we hear that all the cardinals who had known and esteemed Mary had died or had left Rome by the end of 1630, let us not say, "Bad luck!": we are walking in spirit along that stretch of lonely road known to the saints, where God removes all human allies to become Himself the support of His servants. The cardinals at the Holy Office (headquarters of the Inquisition) at this time had never met Mary Ward, and they acted on information supplied by men zealous in the cause of right. Mary was the victim of a genuine seventeenth-century witchhunt.

As soon as the first joyful excitement subsided among the community of the Paradeiser Haus, on reading the papal mandate ordering Mary's release, three of them hastened to the Anger convent, hoping to bring her home with them. It was Friday in Passion Week, the Feast of Our Lady's Dolours, which Mary was spending as a day of recollection, drawing into her heart the graces she would need to remain with the Queen of Sorrows at the foot of the cross, in faithful love, with the dying Christ. She had received so many graces in prayer in the two months she had spent in her wretched cell, that she had been able to write very often at the top of her lemon-juice notes: "From my palace, not prison, for truly so I find it." Now, at the word of release, as Mary Poyntz has her arm round her, she makes her little request: Will they mind very much if she does not go home till Monday? She would like to spend Palm Sunday in this cell as a day of recollection and thanksgiving. Mary Poyntz and her companions could hardly refuse; anyhow, Monday was only a few days off.

Shortly after they had left, Mary received a message from the Elector and Electress asking to see her; for of course Maximilian received a copy of the mandate for her release. Mary wrote immediately to the Paradeiser Haus, asking Elizabeth Cotton to go to the palace and to thank the Electress, and, through her, the Elector; to tell them that she (Mary Ward) is willing to spend Palm Sunday at the Anger ("it being a principal feast with poor me"), but that she will call on her way home on Monday. Then she urges Elizabeth Cotton to ask tactfully if the Electress would send her litter "on Monday at twelve and half, or one, after dinner; but urge it not, by no means."

For twenty-three years Mary had kept Palm Sunday as a feast-day in her heart, because it was on that day in 1608 in Flanders that she had, before leaving the convent of Poor Clares which she herself had founded, dedicated herself to God to do His will, making with that intention a vow of perpetual chastity. As she rededicated herself to His service on this Palm Sunday in 1631, she wasted no thoughts on the hard road she had travelled, but asked for more abundant grace to offer herself completely for the sufferings yet to come. She knew she would return to a convent where the class-rooms and play-grounds were deserted, all the pupils having been withdrawn by their parents at the request of Mary Poyntz. All the girls had looked puzzled; most of them had wept as they said good-bye to the nuns whose own eyes were glistening with tears, belying their consoling words that it was only for a while perhaps, and that they would surely meet again. The school gates had been locked after the last pupil had passed through, and the nuns had returned to the house, making a detour that they might not see the empty class-rooms. Mary Ward knew that this was the aspect of her wrecked life that would strike her at once on her return home. She closed her eyes in pain and acceptance, passing on, though against her will, to the moment when she would tell the community that they were no longer bound by their vows. They must wear secular clothes;

and if any of them wished to return to their home or friends she would help them to prepare for the journey.

On Monday she said good-bye to the Poor Clares and stepped into the carriage that the Electress had sent for her. As she drove along in the open carriage bearing Maximilian's coat-of-arms, and attended by his grooms, she realized that she had done the right thing in arranging such a homecoming. The people in the streets recognized her and bowed to her; she was openly under the protection of the Elector and his wife; and it was important that this should be known as widely as possible, that her companions should not have to bear the stigma of having a heretic as their foundress. Thus was the first faint note struck in the revival of the Institute. But many hard years had to be faced. Mary knew that well; with all the resolution of her courageous heart she applied herself to the task at hand: to comfort and console the community waiting for her now on the front porch of the Paradeiser Haus.

16. Dying into Life

*"I would fain be to the Divine Goodness
what his own hand is to a man."*

(THEOLOGICA GERMANICA)

THE BULL of Suppression broke up the lives of nearly three hundred religious living in the ten houses of the Institute. Many returned to their homes; some entered other orders; others, again, shaken and disillusioned, returned to the pleasures and cares of the world. Thinking of these, particularly, Mary lay awake often far into the night. In those night watches she thought, too, of her faithful Winefrid Wigmore, who also had been imprisoned as a heretic in Liége.

The wording of the Bull left little hope for any revival of the Institute, which was pronounced "suppressed, extinct, uprooted and abolished." But Mary had to show a cheerful face to everyone in the house, and to discuss in a matter-of-fact way even the humbling topic of secular dress. For most of the English members clung to their life with Mary and each other, yet could not wear religious dress. Over the twenty-two years of their life as religious, the original widows' dress had come to have all the appearance of a religious habit; this they must now put aside. A more or less dignified head-dress, such as we see on ladies in some of Rubens' pictures, could be worn in the fashion of the day; but the poverty that enveloped them now in all its rigour could be seen in the cheap dark dresses they had to wear. Nearly all these ladies had come from aristocratic

155

homes in England; and let us not say that they didn't mind the people in the Munich streets looking at them with disdain. Some of the mammas tried to explain to acquaintances: "Yes, it was sad, wasn't it? Such a wonderful school too. You know they were great friends of the Elector Maximilian and his wife? But foreigners are so unpredictable . . . and especially the English." Our heroic English Ladies overheard a great deal of the gossip, and the younger ones among them must have found it almost intolerable.

Besides the loss of the revenue from their schools, the English Ladies felt the pinch of other monetary losses, chief of these being the withdrawal of the yearly grant made by Maximilian when he lent them the Paradeiser Haus on their arrival from Italy in 1626. Punctilious in the matter of obedience to the Holy See, he felt that a yearly grant under the circumstances of the suppression would have the appearance of defiance. So, reluctantly, he withdrew it. But he showed them his friendship by obtaining from the Pope special leave for any who wished to continue living under the roof of the Paradeiser Haus. This had important effects on Catholic education in Bavaria, when the storm of the suppression had abated. But for the present it was merely the hostel for a group of impoverished English ladies. . . . The second factor in their pecuniary distress was their inability to receive money from relatives in England; this was due partly to the persistence of the Penal Laws in England and partly to the confusion caused in Europe by the Thirty Years' War. A few weeks after Mary came home from her imprisonment in the Anger convent, news reached Munich of the great victory of the Catholic general, Tilly, over the Swedes under Gustavus Adolphus at Magdeburg. It seemed then that Bavaria would be spared the horrors of war.

An instance of Mary Ward's supernatural foreknowledge may be seen at this time. She was out of her prison about a week, and there were no indications either that the war would touch Munich or that Maximilian would allow her to continue to live in the Paradeiser Haus. One of the community told her that it was being said in Munich that they would be ejected from the Haus and also from the city. When Mary heard the rumour she said quietly: "This will not happen. I and mine shall remain in this house; but the Elector will be driven from his palace." In something over a year's time Gustavus Adolphus marched upon Munich, remaining in possession of the city for over three weeks. Maximilian and the Electress had to flee from their palace. For more than two years the Swedish soldiers held Munich as their headquarters while they ravaged the whole of Bavaria, leaving the country a scene of desolation. To the horrors of war—massacre and starvation—were added the horrors of the plague. The ladies in the Paradeiser Haus suffered from such poverty that they were often on the verge of starvation. They had often to beg for their food or for an alms to buy it with, and no account of these days would be complete without the mention of the Bavarian lay-sister, Anna Rörlin—"my Jungfrau," as Mary affectionately called her—who used to go on long begging expeditions out into the country, occupied in many cases by foreign soldiery, and bring home food for the family in the Paradeiser Haus.

To return to Mary Ward's personal history: After her return to her community in the Paradeiser Haus in April 1631, the first members of the suppressed Institute to arrive came from Vienna, where the Emperor Ferdinand had reluctantly said good-bye to them. He held out as long as he could against the edict of suppression but finally had to let the English

Ladies leave their flourishing schools which he had equipped
with such munificence. He kept the Bull of Suppression private, thus sparing the sisters the humiliation endured by their
companions in Munich. But no matter how warmly the Munich
sisters welcomed them—there were about sixty of them—it
was a melancholy reunion. Mary Ward had to go through all
the details with them as she had with the Munich community.
. . . At last, when the house was tolerably settled, she and her
advisers turned their attention to the important matter of re-
habilitating the good name of Mary Ward. She had been released from prison, it was true, but the stigma of heresy still
adhered to her name, and, through her, besmirched the good
name of all the English Ladies. So in council it was decided
that Mary should go to Rome to see the Pope. Her enemies
must have guessed that that would be her course, for two
messages for her arrived from the Holy Office. The first said
that as she was so delicate, she should not undertake any journey but should remain in Munich. The second message showed
that her enemies felt she would persuade the Pope to let her
journey to Rome, for she was ordered to come to Rome at
her own expense, to be accompanied by a Commissary appointed by the Dean, and to arrive by a given date. These con-
tradictory messages were sardonically received by Mary's
councillors in the Paradeiser Haus, and she appealed directly
to Pope Urban:

Most Holy Father,—If, through my poor labours, undertaken and
wholly directed, as far as it was in me, without any other view or
interest, to the greater service of Holy Church and of the Apostolic See, I have more or less displeased your Holiness, prostrate at
your sacred feet, I most humbly ask pardon, and entreat you by
the mercy of God to deign with paternal affection to forgive all

that in which, without knowing it or without any will of mine, I may have offended you. Or if a greater punishment be judged necessary than publicly to be declared a heretic, a schismatic, an obstinate rebel against Holy Church; to be taken and imprisoned as such; to have been at the gates of death through the inconveniences endured for nine weeks; to have been deprived of the Holy Sacraments from the 7th of February (when I was taken) until the 28th of March, when I had my Viaticum, and two days after the Holy Oils; to be held up to obloquy in all places both as guilty of so great wickedness, and thrown by orders of Holy Church into the jaws of death for such enormities—if more is needed than the sufferings of all in our company, ridiculed by the heretics at the present time for having left their country and parents, despised by Catholics, held as disgraced by their nearest relations, their annual revenues unjustly taken from them, so that in four of our colleges ours are obliged to beg their bread, and many other sufferings already endured by individuals amongst us—if all this is too little, I offer my poor and short life. . . .

The rest of the letter deals with the plan, proposed by the Dean, for her journey to Rome. (He was only an intermediary, of course.) Mary encloses a copy of the plan forwarded to her from "the Lord Cardinals of the Sacred Congregation of the Holy Office." . . . She was wise in thus appealing personally to the Pope, who must have answered her immediately, for at the end of April 1632 we find her setting out for Rome, quite at liberty as to the conditions of her journey, and with Elizabeth Cotton and Anne Turner as her companions. Faithful Robert busied himself with the simple preparations for the journey, but Father Lee is absent this time. On Mary's advice, he had accepted an offer of a canonry at the Munich cathedral when they were no longer allowed a chaplain at the Paradeiser Haus. But Robert and he discussed every aspect of this third and last journey of Mary to Rome. They were especially anxious that she should make no delay about her departure, for Munich was in a turmoil with the war news, that Gustavus Adolphus had entered Bavaria and was confident of soon conquering the capital. This he did when Mary and her companions were halfway to Rome.

They followed the same route as that taken by Mary on her first journey from Rome to Munich in 1626. In spite of their shabby clothes (browns and greys being now seen in their wardrobe) a kind and respectful welcome was accorded them at Parma and Florence, where the honour given to the pilgrims was as great as before, even though subdued now in the presence of suffering that had left its searing marks on the features of Mary Ward. The charm of her smile still lit up her eyes, now deeply shadowed by ill-health and weariness; and as she told of extraordinary escapes from dangers in the hilly country of the Tyrol, her princely hosts and hostesses realized that this charming woman must not be questioned about the happenings in Munich. They were her own sorrow. Smiling and grateful, she left her hosts, her passing like a benediction upon them.

Between Florence and Rome the party encountered no dangers to spoil their enjoyment of the beauty of the Tuscan landscape, now in the full flush of springtime flowering. Wild flowers dotted the fields in profusion; and in the hilly country the fresh greens of the young vines could be seen on every slope, with patches of plane trees and birches, their new leaves showing against the darker greens of cypress and ilex and the grey-greens of the olive groves. The road passed blossomy orchards lying on the outskirts of white villages nestling in valleys or clinging to mountain ridges. Mary arranged the journey to have Mass every morning if possible; most often this would be in a little Romanesque church with a beautiful façade. They would pass through its simple portal wrought in pure rounded-arch style; and as they went down the aisle after Mass their eyes would be drawn upwards to the single rose window glowing like a multi-coloured jewel, its beauty touching a chord in their English hearts as they thought of their own lovely churches, beautiful still, but empty shells without the Mass. In those days English Catholics had an inevitable destiny of homesickness, their faith and their country being two loves sundered by a sea of blood.

In Rome they found quiet lodgings where Elizabeth Cotton and Anne insisted on a few days of rest for Mary before her audience with Pope Urban. Before the week was out Mary and Elizabeth were on their way to the Vatican; this time there were no preparations, no memorial to be drawn up—the time for formalities had passed. Mary was in Rome to plead like a child with the Holy Father. There was still a barb in her heart, and only he could draw it out. She, Mary Ward, kinswoman of martyrs and devoted child of the Church, had been imprisoned by the Inquisition as a heretic. For the thousandth time she turned her mind away from the bitter thought and tried to compose an eloquent speech, only to reject it as soon as composed. . . .

Here she was at the Vatican, and she had no idea what she was going to say. As she walked along the gallery to the audience chamber she calmed her heart in prayer; the Holy Spirit would guide her. The door opened, then closed behind her, and she saw Pope Urban seated at his table. . . .

Mary went swiftly towards the Pope, and falling at his feet she clasped her hands and looked up at him: "Holy Father, I neither am nor ever have been a heretic." Urban took her hands in his, and spoke at once: "We believe it, We believe it; We need no other proof. We and the Cardinals are well informed as to yourself, and your habits, and your exemplary conduct. We and they all are not only satisfied, but edified; and We know that you have carried on your Institute well. We have nevertheless permitted the trial of your virtues, nor must you think it much to have been proved as you have been, as other Popes, Our predecessors, have done in similar cases, who have exercised the endurance of the servants of God."

Mary next asked for the release of Winefrid Wigmore. This was the first the Pope heard of her imprisonment, and he heard it with displeasure, promising that he would give immediate orders for her release. Then came the request that had been the subject of many earnest talks between Mary and her counsellors before she set out for Rome: the future of the Institute. Mary realized that it would have to be from the original simplicity, if from anything, that the Institute would make a fresh start—just she and a group of English ladies living as a family to help in the education of girls wherever they were needed, without any talk for the present of a confirmed Rule. As her thoughts flew to those English ladies—some of them now middle-aged women—who were depending on her in the Paradeiser Haus, she took her courage in her hands and spoke her fears and her anxious sense of responsibility in their regard. Urban listened attentively and asked her had she any plan for them. On hearing from Mary that they would like to come to Rome to live under her guidance and under the protection of the Holy See, he said at once: "Yes, We are glad that they should come, and We will take them under our protection."

Mary's enemies in Rome were not slow to learn that she had taken a large house in the city and that a party of English Ladies from Bavaria was expected to come into residence there within a few months. On the extravagant supposition that these ladies would spend most of their time at the papal court, the "Jerusalems" persuaded some one in authority at the Vatican to draw Urban's attention to such a menace to papal decorum. But Urban dismissed the matter without discussion, merely saying that he had given the permission and that it was his wish that they should come. He summoned some of his own relatives and committed to their care Mary Ward and any English Ladies living with her. His sister-in-law, the Princess Constanza, received her commission with delight, as she had been worrying over her inability to do anything to help her friend. Her daughter, Anna, was also given the duty of being a friend and companion to the English Ladies, while the Pope's two nephews, who were cardinals, were recommended to watch over their interests so that the malice of their enemies might not touch them. Such were the happy conditions in which Mary welcomed the large party from Munich who arrived, after delays caused by the winter and the war, in May 1633.

At Urban's request Constanza lent them one of her carriages, and her daughter introduced the whole party, three at a time, into his presence. He spoke to each one with fatherly kindness, telling them that their coming to Rome gave him much pleasure, and that he was sure everyone would be edified by their way of living. When the "Jerusalems" saw how their machinations were failing, they made one more attempt—one more, for the present—to prevent Mary from gathering this group of countrywomen about her. A prelate in sympathy with these clerics conveyed their fear to the Pope that if the Ladies were allowed to live with Mary, the Bull would be nullified. But Urban was firm, giving his final answer in the form of a pertinent question: "Where would they live, or where could they live so well?"

17. Mary's Last Italian Years

"Havremo a caro che venghino e ne terremo protettione."[1]

(POPE URBAN VIII TO MARY WARD)

WHEN MARY obtained permission from Urban for the English ladies at the Paradeiser Haus to join her in Rome, she was thinking especially of the group of nine girls who had arrived in Munich in 1629 to enter the novitiate. They were at once admitted and were still in the novitiate at the time of the suppression in 1631. The eldest was Helen Marshall, who had been twenty-one when she entered the novitiate; the youngest, Frances Bedingfield and Frances Constable—only fourteen years of age. The heroism of their noble and martyred kinsmen is to be seen in their brave and purposeful lives, which not even the disaster of the suppression could deflect into the comfortable ruts of mediocrity. They cheerfully put on their worldly frocks, which they hauled out of the trunk containing the playclothes used by the boarders in their school dramas. Pressed with an iron they looked presentable, though somewhat short, for you are still growing at fifteen. There was no novitiate, but with the resilience of youth they adapted themselves to the family life in which they were the youngest sisters. The brightness of their youth was not the least of their gifts to the suffering Institute. When Mary Ward left for Rome in

[1] "We are glad that they should come, and We will take them under our protection."

1632, she told them she would soon return to Munich; and such faith did they have in her that they felt all would surely work out happily.

The day before Mary's departure had occurred an incident which was to be related to children in Institute schools by these English girls, when in the course of the years they were professed nuns. It happened one day that a handful of peas was the only fare which the cook had to serve up for the dinner. She sent word to Mary of the lean prospect before the family. There was no money in the house to buy more; so Mary, strong in her trust in God, desired that they should be cooked and served round, when to the astonishment of all there was not only enough for everyone, but as many as had been cooked were left in the dish. They all knew better than to exclaim or proclaim on such occasions; they merely followed her example of grateful acquiescence as she said with shining eyes: "How kind and fatherly is our good God."

The next day as they gathered round her to say good-bye, the seniors found it natural that she should give special attention to the English girls so far away from their homes, and so uncomplaining. While recommending the whole household to the motherly care of Mary Poyntz, she drew Frances Constable especially to her side, saying: "And take special care of this one, for she will soon be in heaven." All looked surprised, as Frances was strong and well; and the girl herself, not quite sure if Mother was joking, felt blushes mount to her already rosy cheeks. She died in a few weeks, on the 30th of June, soon after Mary arrived in Rome. . . . When Mary sent to Munich for the other girls, there were only seven out of the nine to come, as Helen Marshall was too ill to be of the party. She died in the following year; the Lord wanted nothing more from her and Frances Constable than their generous oblation in leaving all things to follow Him.

When their seven companions arrived in Rome in 1633, Mary's first thought was of their religious training, lest their gifted lives be frittered away in the amusements that Anna Barberini and her friends would most assiduously provide. Mary felt that an important work had been done when she had them happily settled in the novitiate, where the healing routine of prayer, study, manual work and recreation restored the tranquil silence of their souls so that the Holy Spirit could lead them along the ways of divine love. At first Mary herself attended to much of their training, foreseeing that they would be the fresh growth in her new Institute. One day about this time when Mary was walking along a gallery near the novitiate she saw a novice dusting a balustrade. Something about the line of her neck and shoulders (or was it the listless droop of the duster?) told Mary that all was not well. One look at the discontented young face confirmed her fears: fervour was waning, and everything seemed difficult. The girl cried a little when she saw that Mary read her soul; cried from relief rather than any other emotion—she had dreaded telling anyone that she felt she could not go on with this monotonous life. (And how monotonous it can be at times, until God establishes us, beyond our moods, in the quiet pastures of His peace.) Mary said affectionately: "My dear child, virtue is only hard to those who think it to be so. . . . Your way to heaven must be to receive everything from the hand of God, and to seek Him in all." The novice smiled, all tension gone, and Mary resumed her walk. In a few minutes the duster was industriously threading the banisters, though withdrawn occasionally to flick away a happy tear. . . . The following year the novice was professed with her fellow-novices in the Basilica of Sta. Maria Maggiore which Urban had specially selected for the religious ceremony of their vows.[2]

The house in Rome where Mary and her companions finally settled was on the Esquiline not far from Sta. Maria Maggiore; the location, a happy one as the basilica was especially dear to Mary. There she and Winefrid Wigmore went to make a visit of thanksgiving when at last reunited on Winefrid's return from her prison at Liége. No one knows anything of what happened, or of how Winefrid lived during that lamentable miscarriage of justice. She was the only one who could have written it down, but her self-effacement would not allow any record to be kept. She visited Urban to thank him for her release and for the joy of living again with Mary Ward. They were to remain together now to the very end in a friendship the heavenly light of which shone on the whole household; no one could ever be jealous of Winefrid Wigmore. A certain timidity made her dislike holding office, and she was glad when her friend consented to call Mary Poyntz from Munich to be Superior and novice-mistress of the Roman house. All this may sound as if a great deal of money were changing hands, but the truth is that the small community in Munich was just as desperately poor as the Roman one.

To enable them to live, Mary obtained permission from Urban to take, as pupils and boarders, daughters of English *émigrés* who were crowding into Rome. Many of these people had left their country not to escape the Penal Laws but to get away before the Revolution broke over them. By 1635 it was pretty clear in England that the high-handed methods of King

---

[2] Frances Bedingfield made her vows at this time, and was then sent with a companion to work in London.

Charles were driving the country to civil war, and that the Scotch Presbyterians and English Parliamentarians were one in opposing the autocracy of Charles. Many of the aristocracy, both Catholic and Protestant, who had hung about the Stuart court, now, reading the signs of the times, packed up and crossed the Channel. Where their means permitted, they travelled as far as Rome. They were not cast in the heroic mould. It has been one of the tragedies in English history after the Reformation that the Catholics who gathered round the Stuart sovereigns were, on the whole, a worldly crowd to whom their religion meant little. They had done rather well with Charles I whose wife, Henrietta Maria, was a Catholic; this at least gave them a certain prestige at court, saving them also from the fear of having to face martyrdom. In Rome the *émigrés*, Protestant as well as Catholic, were not long in finding the house of Mary Ward, whose charity embraced them all, though she found it in her heart to wish that they had stayed to help Charles through the storm that was breaking over him. (She could never forget that night of prayer for him in the church at Feldkirch.)

Several of the men-folk of these families had already visited Rome, for that was the crowning achievement of every well-educated young Englishman in the seventeenth century. To him was valid the trilogy, Roma: Italia: Il Mondo. He would set off from London with his tutor to do the grand tour, and it was only a few years before the time of which we write that the poet Milton was walking about Rome, where the Church has preserved for her own use, and for travellers' joy, almost all that was best in paganism. Painters and sculptors as well as writers from all nations travelled to Rome, the mother of learning and the arts. Here the French painters Claude and

Poussin could have been seen by Mary Ward, had she known where they were putting up their easels to set down on canvas the charm of the countryside with its classic background that was to haunt them ceaselessly when they returned to France. In their landscapes the Baroque century found its best expression. The Flemish painter, Van Dyck, at this time court painter to Charles I in England, had also left pictures in Roman galleries to be mementoes of his visit. These were eagerly hunted up by the English *émigrés*, some of whom had been painted by him; others, less affluent, had at least a Van Dyck collar—or two—in their wardrobe. . . . The Roman painters themselves, at this time painting in their studios, numbered in their ranks Carlo Dolci, Domenichino, Gherardo Della Notte, Giordano, Guido Reni and Sassoferrato. Maratta was still a boy, but the studios were still haunted by the genius of Barocci. Little wonder that every artist felt he had to go to Rome in the early seventeenth century no matter where he lived.

The *epoca Barocca*, as the Italians call it, was in the exuberance of its flowering in the first half of the seventeenth century with its architects and sculptors, Maderna, Bernini, Borromini and Cortona. All of these had worked on the magnificent Palazzo Barberini, which was built for Cardinal Maffeo Barberini before he became Pope Urban VIII. The chattering knots of English women gathered in Mary Ward's reception rooms in her house on the Esquiline. The critical ladies learnt early to keep their gossip on impersonal subjects when in the hearing of Mary Ward. But everything beautiful became more beautiful to the beholders if shared with her, even Bernini's latest work of genius, the *baldacchino*, that gorgeous creation in bronze with its twisted columns covered with golden bees.

At this time Rome was also the centre of the musical world.

The older Romans still remembered the music in St. Peter's and Santa Maria Maggiore while Palestrina was at the height of his powers. But now his rarefied polyphony had given way to the Baroque ornamentation that became the fashion in church music. A great deal had happened in the Roman world of music in thirty years. Nowhere was this more noticed than in St. Peter's, where the composer and organist Frescobaldi was drawing audiences of thirty thousand people. His style was typical of the era, for while he was a master of the older polyphonic forms, of fugue and chorale variation, he was also an inventive genius expressing himself in brilliant improvisations marked by rich and varied harmony. The English *émigrés*, whose musical training had been on austere lines, responded according to temperament as they listened to the rhapsodic freedom of Frescobaldi, whose music seemed to pour in cascades from the organ loft in St. Peter's. . . . In the field of secular music the name of Monteverdi was spoken everywhere in Italy. He himself was at this time choir-master at St. Mark's in Venice; but before going there he had laid the foundations in Rome of Italian opera, with its songs, dances and marches and all the romantic glamour which became the permanent atmosphere of the opera. As early as 1608 Monteverdi had an orchestra of thirty-six pieces, mainly strings. By the time of which we write the Romans were intoxicated with the opera; and to say that most of the English *émigrés* found it delightful is merely to repeat an expression of their own controlled exuberance. In Mary Ward's reception rooms they discussed, applauded—or demurred if they felt the need of keeping their heads. Their gracious hostess was never censorious, but to individuals in her vicinity, whether they were English or Italians, she would sometimes say: *Tutto passa.* Yes,

indeed, everything passes, passes like the wind: *come il vento.*
. . . Gradually those men and women who really needed her
friendship came in ones or twos to talk with her, hoping to
draw into their restless hearts the peace that shone from her
eyes.

The spies of the Inquisition, never far away from Mary
during those last years in Italy, observed the comings and
goings by the front door of the house on the Esquiline. Again,
an accommodating prelate undertook for them the delicate
matter of complaining of Mary Ward to Urban: All kinds of
peculiar English visitors were constantly with her. But Urban
was not alarmed; he even smiled with sympathy as he said that
he was very glad to hear it, "for assuredly they are either very
good or they will become so, since they frequent that house."
So, Mary and her companions went their way, and when Mary
Poyntz arrived from Munich she found a settled regime over
which she became Superior. Her place in Munich was taken
by Winefrid Bedingfield, for Barbara Babthorpe had her
hands full as Provincial. (Of course, the terms Provincial and
Superior were not used after the suppression.) Mary Poyntz
brought good news that Barbara had obtained leave from the
Elector Maximilian to reopen a school, as private citizens who
must have some revenue unless they were to become beggars.
Except the news that Winefrid Wigmore brought from Liége,
little was known of what was going on in Flanders. How glad
they would have been could they have seen the letter that
Urban had ordered the Secretary of the Holy Office to send
off to the Nuncio at Cologne:

There are in this city, at the present time, the Lady Donna
Maria della Guardia[3] with some other of her English companions,

3 The Italian form of her name, used in Italy by Mary Ward.

who with acts of humility and of fitting reverence towards the Holy See, have most readily obeyed what our Holy Lord commanded concerning the suppression of their Institute, to the entire satisfaction of their Eminences, my lords. To whom it has appeared good that I should make you acquainted with this result, to the end that if from evil-disposed or badly-informed persons you should hear the contrary, you may attest to them this truth. Also, that if you should be questioned, you may affirm that in this holy tribunal, the English Ladies who have lived under the Institute of Donna Maria della Guardia, are not found, nor ever have been found, guilty of any failure which regards the holy and orthodox Catholic faith. . . .

The letter then orders that all the properties that have been taken "with injustice" from the same Ladies shall be restored to them, that each one may have the wherewithal to live in the world where they find themselves.

Another letter written about the same time, but from England, would have caused them wry amusement. It was from a "Jerusalem" to a colleague then living in Paris, and ran:

Mrs. Ward is said here to be gone up to Rome with a certainty of having her order confirmed; but, as I hear, the Fathers advise her to lay down her imaginary pretended mission, and to apply her aim only to a confirmation of her Institute to bring up feminine youth, so by that means, between them, both sexes shall have a general dependence on them. This project will prove as dangerous to the Church, and particularly all orders of that sex, as their other project was ridiculous. . . .

But Mary did not see that letter with its perennial "bogy" of her secret co-operation with the Jesuits. It would have sounded in her ears like a grim jest, broken as she still was from her imprisonment as a heretic in Munich, where the

Rector of the Jesuit College, Father Contzen, had boasted that he had "done the deed" of manoeuvring the charge against her.

The annoying espionage of the Inquisition, kept at boiling point by the "Jerusalems," extended even to the capture of letters that Mary wrote and received. Referring to the loss of letters in transit, Mary remarked in a note to the sisters in Munich: "Perchance we serve not the angel of our letters as we should." Knowing that their letters might be read by hostile eyes, they used disguised names and forms of expression. Mary calls herself sometimes Felice, at other times Phillis; sometimes Margery, and often just "the old woman." Money is "yellow silk," the "loom" is the new house opened in Rome. Mary's correspondents have to recognize themselves under the names Ned, Peter, Will. The Pope is generally Antony. Back and forth went the strange little notes between Munich and Rome; and it is in them that we recognize the great poverty that beset both houses at this time; recognize also the sisterly charity that bound them. It was often on the backs of the letters written by Winefrid Wigmore or Mary Poyntz that Mary Ward wrote her affectionate little notes, so humanly worded even in their seventeenth-century style:

"I cannot easily scribble worse than this good woman hath done, my dear Winn. Be wholly God's and keep to your utmost all He hath given yourself or left in your charge. How happy a thing it is to love God and serve and seek Him *da vero*. I do not now answer your loving and good letter of the 22nd of 7ber. I am hindered; and betwixt us needs no more, I may be bold. *Vale*." To the end of their lives, Winefrid Bedingfield and Barbara Babthorpe in Munich treasured these little scribbles. At another time it was a greeting that ended: "Be merry, good and happy; and pray for her that never forgets you. I give you not a word of thanks for your money, nor tell you the much service it hath done. *Vale, vale.*" Often her affectionate heart could hardly express its love: "I ever loved much more than ordinary; but I shall fear to love you too much, if your proceedings be still such as I verily think they will. *Vale.*"

As the year 1635 advanced, Mary's health deteriorated to an alarming degree, as we see in a letter from Mary Poyntz to Munich: "My dear Mother's health is most poor; she is even lame besides all other pains." By the middle of the year it was so bad that the physicians ordered her to the waters at San Cassiano. The spies in Rome viewed this move with disfavour, for they had been giving out reports for some months that she was merely a prisoner at large in Rome, suffered to live there on parole but not permitted to leave it. When they heard that she was quietly preparing to go to San Cassiano as a perfectly free agent they had a report sent in to Urban, along their usual channel, declaring that she really intended to go to England by way of San Cassiano, and that if she were allowed to do this, great ill-effects to the Church in England would result. Urban's timidity was so worked upon by their arguments that he sent a prelate attached to his household to give Mary a message from himself, to the effect that, for certain reasons of state, he preferred she should not leave Rome for the present.

The prelate, Monsignor Boccabella, gave the message, which Mary received with that mixture of firmness and gentleness so peculiarly her own: "Am I then a prisoner?" "By no means," he answered, "you are free, entirely free; nor is there anything in you that is held in suspicion, and I myself am a witness of the paternal tenderness and affection which his Holiness has for you; but there are considerations for which he wishes that you should not go out of Rome." But Mary could not let the matter rest at that unsatisfactory point; so she said with great earnestness: "This is a difficult matter. My life and my good name, which I value more than life, are here both concerned. I know how far duty obliges me in such a case; yet, tell his Holiness from me that I am most ready to obey him, and that I lay them both at his feet not only willingly but with devotion, and that I would willingly sacrifice a thousand lives if I had them in order to obey his wishes." Monsignor Boccabella's eyes glistened with tears as he heard her; he pressed her hand for a second in friendship before hastily going on his way to Urban, who was so impressed by his description of Mary, that he sent word at once to those concerned that "She should go whither she would and as she would." So Winefrid Wigmore made the final arrangements for the trip to San Cassiano.

The place was crowded with visitors in search of health at its mineral waters. As Mary filled her glass at the fountain the morning after her arrival, a priest in a religious habit stood not far away. Mary pointed him out to Winefrid, saying quietly: "He is put to be my spy." Winefrid dared not even look, so dismayed did she feel. When they were by themselves, she asked for particulars, but Mary merely answered, "Do not fear; God will help us; we will so pray to his good angel, that he shall not have the power to say anything in prejudice of God's honour, or our innocency." Two days later, the priest sickened and died.

These priests were not bad men; most of them genuinely believed that Mary was a dangerous innovator. If they were foreigners, they knew nothing about England except that it was a country where heresy had triumphed. As for the English Clergy agents, who more readily than we should forgive them? for their great desire was the restoration of the Catholic faith to England. Exiles from their country, they were the victims of its Penal Laws, which had hunted them with persistent malignancy, warping characters that were unfitted for heroic ways. Persecution of itself does not make saints; and on less exacting paths these men would probably have done well their daily task. Something of a similar twisting of character into over-sensitiveness and suspicion may be seen in our own day in men who have spent some years in enemy concentration camps. If we are to share at all in the spirit of Mary Ward, we must allow our charity to cover all those whom she herself forgave; and not only forgave, but *loved*, so that people said of her that it was "better to be her enemy than her friend."

Not far from San Cassiano were hills where some of the Roman nobility had their country homes. Among these was the beautiful château of the Marchese de Monte, a friend of Mary Ward. The Marchese placed the whole castle at the disposal of Mary, who was too ill even for the effort of "taking the waters." It was one of those magnificent Renaissance country homes that belonged especially to Italy. Near the small town of Piano Castagnano, it could have been the only dwelling in the world, so complete was its seclusion. Mary's small party occupied three or four rooms out of the total of three hundred, and without leaving the grounds they could wander about in untouched woodland. Sometimes as they sat resting in chairs on a shaded marble terrace they would hear across the valleys the horns of huntsmen. One day as they listened to the sounds floating over the valleys, the keeper of the castle presented himself to Mary to say that the Spanish Ambassador to the Tuscan Court was out hunting, and, as he was a special friend of the Marchese, he would like to rest at the castle for a few hours. But the keeper said he had been told by his master to admit no one without the permission of the Lady Donna Maria della Guardia. She at once gave permission.

Realizing that her health would greatly benefit by a sojourn in pure mountain air, Mary accepted the Marchese's invitation to remain there for some weeks; and then made arrangements for a confessor and chaplain. She chose a Franciscan priest from the friary in Piano Castagnano; all she knew of him was that he was a man of singular learning and exemplary life. She learnt after she left that he was an Inquisitor specially appointed at Piano Castagnano to spy on her. Being the kind of man he was, he must have felt dismayed when he received her unsuspecting message asking him to be her confessor. He could not refuse, and how strangely must have read his report sent in to Rome some months later, after he had learnt of the inner life of Mary Ward. It is said that the account he wrote of her "was sufficient not only for her justification, but even for her canonization."

Strengthened by the nourishing food and quiet regime at the castle, Mary returned to continue the cure at San Cassiano, where she found the crowds of health-seekers still gathering and dispersing around the fountains of mineral waters or going off to the baths. Holiday-makers who were gregariously inclined found the recuperative routine very pleasant. In Mary's absence they had discussed her as they stood, beakers in hand, sipping with puckered mouths at the bitter waters. Her history was an intriguing topic and lent itself to thorough discussion, in which the old stagers took the lead, pooling their observations and recalling titbits they had heard in Rome. The result was a fairly accurate appraisement of Mary's present position. That Mary and Winefrid had been making holiday at the castle of the Marchese de Monte made them even more interesting in the eyes of the vivacious Tuscans, who now welcomed them with much pleasure, which increased to affectionate sympathy for Mary when the whisper began to pass among them that this gentle and saintly Englishwoman was the victim of a web of espionage. Great was the indignation of the Tuscans at hearing the names of the towns where spies were posted. All in Tuscany! They told Mary that the hated Inquisition had never been allowed a footing in Tuscany, and that they would give her money and other aid to fight it. The prospect of such an engagement so alarmed her that she begged them to put their minds on something else. Relieved by their agreement with her wishes, she allowed herself that evening, with Winefrid, in the privacy of her room, the luxury of delighted laughter. Her sense of humour often released the tension on her overworked nerves.

The rumours about the posted spies were no idle chatter of the watering-place, for a few days after Mary's return to San Cassiano a priest in a religious habit asked if he might speak with her; he seemed disturbed. The burden of his words was that a certain member of his own order had been appointed to be her spy at San Cassiano on her first arrival, that he had died not long after that—yes, he was the one Mary had seen— and that, as soon as she had left Rome, word had been sent appointing Inquisitors in several towns to the north, to prevent her from going to England. The priest was obviously nervous as he told Mary these things, and he begged her not to disclose his name. He said that after observing her for some days he was so edified by her conduct and so completely convinced of her innocence that his conscience would give him no rest until he warned her of her danger. (We may here remark that

Mary's persecutors were always people who had never met her; she was the victim of hearsay.)

Shortly after this Mary returned to Rome to her community, where her improved health was matter for prayerful gratitude; the novices managed this part of it with zest. They did not know that Mary was worried by spies; her charming conversation when she came to their recreation showed nothing of her anxiety. . . . The next morning by appointment she was admitted to the presence of Urban in the Vatican. This business of espionage must be discussed. Kneeling at his feet she said: "Holy Father, what more can poor Mary Ward do to prove her fidelity and loyalty towards your Holiness and towards the Catholic Church; but must her life, her good name and her liberty also be left in the hands of men, but too easily suborned and corrupted?" Urban, with fatherly kindness, allowed her to end the sentence before saying: "Be satisfied, my daughter, it shall be so no more; henceforth, no one will be able to wrong you with us, in the least. In the process of information given we found both malice and folly." From then on Mary was left in peace, to go or come as she would. (Looking now, three hundred years later, at Bernini's magnificent Fountain of the Triton in the plaza before the Palazzo Barberini, a thought persists: Was not Maffeo Barberini, considered as a figure of history rather than as pope, so occupied with beautifying Rome that he did not see the petty machinations—so foreign to his own princely character—that were being pursued by the Holy Office in the name of religion?)

That visit in 1635 to Urban was the last time Mary saw him, as far as we know. He kept his word faithfully in putting an end to the annoyances of espionage and showed further proofs of his friendship by increasing the pension he had allowed her

since the break-up of her schools in Rome in 1625. In smaller
matters he also showed his generosity, by ordering that special
medicinal wine be constantly supplied to her and that a carriage from his own stables should always be at her disposal,
though there is no record that she ever made use of it. The
boon above all others was the freedom from persecuting spies;
and, except for renewed bodily pain, the whole of the year
1636 passed without much anxiety. There seemed no reason
now why she should not go to England, as she could safely
leave the house in Rome under the care of Mary Poyntz. But
before she could make any preparations her illness became
acute. When Urban heard of her state he ordered his own physician to attend her and asked Princess Constanza to see that
Mary wanted for nothing. But the illness was desperate; from
the 2nd of January 1637 until March 13, she could not move
from her bed, where she endured paroxysms of pain day and
night. When she recovered somewhat, the physicians, thinking that sea air might restore her, had her carried by litter to
Nettuno. As Urban was informed of her progress and the physicians' orders, he asked the governor of the sea-side town to
show Mary every attention.

Improved in health, she was back in Rome in June; but the
great heat of July undid all the good of the sea breezes at
Nettuno. This time her illness reduced her to the door of
death and she received the Last Sacraments. That afternoon
as she lay in extreme weakness, Cardinal St. Onofrio, Urban's
brother, arrived to give her the Pope's last blessing, which he
delivered with great feeling. Later, in the guest-room, he con-
doled with the sisters on their loss; then, seeming to recover
himself, said that "we were to bless God for having left her to
us for so many years, until she, by word and example, had

made others capable of governing us in her absence." (We have this on the word of Mary Poyntz.)

Mary Ward lay as if dying until the 10th of August, when after a night of great pain she said to Winefrid Wigmore, who was watching beside her bed, that she would go to Spa. To *Spa*, across Europe! Winefrid thought she was delirious, and showed her thoughts; Mary, observing, said: "No, I am not out of myself, but I will go to Spa. I do not myself know what God will do by it; but, humanly speaking, here I must die. There I may recover." . . . In those long hours when fever seemed to recede, leaving her mind free to think, how often had her thoughts not turned to England? It was her homing heart that spoke now. Winefrid must have felt it in her tones, for she made no more argument than to say: "But how for the wherewithal?" To which Mary replied: "God will provide." Then she summoned Barbara Babthorpe from Munich to take her place in Rome.

Urban was agreeable to her plan if she could muster enough health to make the journey. (Her enemies solicitously told him that she was too delicate for such a long journey; but he waved aside their obsessive suspicions.) As she was too ill to visit Urban, Mary Poyntz and Winefrid Wigmore went in her stead to say good-bye and ask for his blessing. When they repeated to him Mary's argument for going he said: "It is true that, humanly speaking, the journey must needs kill her, without hope of escape. But she is a great servant of God; He will guide her to do what is best, and we know not what He would do by her. We will give orders to all our Nuncios where she will pass to receive her, where she must stay and rest herself by the way and as long as she will. For we do esteem her, not only as a woman of great prudence and of extraordinary courage and powers of mind, but what is much more, we consider her as a holy and great servant of God. You who go with her obey and serve her; for as long as you do this you will do well." They were now ready for the road, and the long good-bye to Italy.[4]

[4] Mary Poyntz was to return to Rome in 1654 as successor to Barbara Babthorpe in the office of Superior General.

18. The Exile Goes Home

"Be unwearied; thou art shortly to die and thy reward shall be great."

(OUR LORD'S WORDS TO MARY WARD)

THE ROMAN heat of 1637 gave way at last to a day of early autumn rain that pattered softly on the city streets. Mary had no preparations to make for her journey except a few farewells at her bedside to each member of her household. The promise of a temporary absence softened the anguish of parting, especially for those who were to be left to go in spirit over that long journey beside the litter of their suffering foundress and friend. To each of the young English sisters who came to her bedside there was a private word of encouragement and love, for her own intrepid spirit saluted the brave impulses of their exiled youth. She received all their messages for the loved English home-folk—some of them living in Flanders and France to ensure that their children should have a Catholic education.

When the rain had ceased the portress announced that the bearers were at the street door ready for the journey. Mary was wrapped warmly in blankets and carried downstairs to be placed in the litter. Rugs were tucked round her, and Mary gave a special smile to her cousin, Robert Wright, efficient but self-effacing as ever as he came forward, glad in his quiet way that Mary would be depending on him during the hazards of the journey. His own spiritual stature had grown in the years

184

THE EXILE GOES HOME

of his obscure service, when in silence and prayer he contrib-
uted the support of his own sanctity to the apostolate that
had called him in the strength of his young manhood. . . .
The litter moved off; there were a few last gestures of farewell to the group at the door, and the travellers were on their
way. It was the 10th of September.

Out on the country roads the white dust had been pleasantly
laid by the recent rain, and the hills stood out with luminous
beauty in the rain-washed atmosphere. The curtains were
drawn back on the litter, and Mary was propped up with pillows to enjoy the invigorating air of the country. At night
the party stopped at one of the white villages that beckoned to
them in every hidden valley of the foothills. The morning
came when they saw their last sunrise over the Sabine hills.
Each day they saw to their right the Umbrian highlands, where
Mary, in one far-off and prosperous day, had founded a house
at Perugia. . . . Did she think of it now as her eyes turned
towards the violet Umbrian hills? She had often been on this
road before when going to and from San Cassiano, or as far
abroad as Munich, and she reviewed those journeys now without bitterness or regret, in that kaleidoscopic functioning of
memory that is part of convalescence. Her companions were
glad to see her growing stronger, and occasionally the litter
would pause, that she might take some exercise in the sunshine
or in the chequered shade of the chestnut-woods where the
domed trees were becoming like canopies of red-gold as summer yielded to autumn.

Then one day they saw, rising from a blue background of
Tuscan hills, towers that told them they were approaching
Siena. This was to be their first resting-place. Now their road
lay upwards, sometimes between vineyards noisy with the

industry of the vintage season, sometimes by slopes of ripe wheat ready for the sickle; and often our travellers had to share the road with a team of white oxen with such widely spreading horns that they were always sure of being left plenty of room as they moved along slowly with their lumbering wagon. Beautiful villas, many of them looking like castles, stood back from the road, their white stone towers and porches set off by the dark cypress groves beside or beyond them, and their gardens studded with brilliant patches of oleanders covered with crimson blossoms. As the sun went down behind the hills, the luminous blue that is often seen in valleys on autumn evenings hung like a veil over the foothills before the white city of Siena, just as St. Catherine must have seen it as she journeyed home ill and weary after a visit to Rome. She lived three hundred years before Mary Ward, but there is a remarkable likeness between the two women; and as Mary passed through the southern gates of Siena in the quiet autumn twilight, we like to think that the spirit of the Sienese saint whispered encouragement to her, repeating words that Our Lord Himself had said: "The soul that loves My truth never leaves herself any rest but ever seeks to serve others."

A Tuscan nobleman and his wife had prepared a welcome for Mary when they heard she was to come their way; for by the year 1637 she had friends in all the cities on the road from Rome. As in the case of St. Catherine, her terrible illnesses and her astonishing seasons of recovery were not the least miraculous aspect of her life of charity. For the first few days in Siena, she was ill with a fever; and the physician who was called in said she must certainly "be bled"; so he made an incision in her thin, bloodless arm, leaving her much worse than he found her. Surely the most dangerous incident in a patient's life in those days was the doctor's visit. Having escaped from that hazard, Mary rallied, recovered and spent a strenuous week in advising and consoling those who came to her with their worries. She made a last visit to the cathedral, mounting its steps of yellow marble to enter the prayerful shade where Duccio's Madonna looked sweetly down on those who came to worship her divine Son. . . . As Mary and her companions passed out through the northern gates of Siena, the Angelus bells of noonday rang out from every church, as St. Catherine had often heard them when she set out on her travels; she, too, a pilgrim for souls though she had loved her cell.

A few more days of wayfaring and the travellers were approaching Florence, where they stayed as the guests of Robert Dudley, Duke of Northumberland, whose grandfather had been a political exile. The noble Florentine families vied with each other in offering Mary hospitality but the Duke proudly said that she and her companions were his guests.

To the last day of their visit, they seemed to him like beings strayed from another world, moving him to a dissatisfaction with his idle life. Until he realized that all he had to do as their host was to receive visits on Mary's behalf from the Florentine nobility, he tried several times to be the humanist host, a role for which he was well fitted after his long acquaintance with the art treasures of Renaissance Florence. He would have been in his element showing her Ghiberti's magnificent bronze doors at the Baptistery of the Duomo, and the sculptured beauties left by Donatello, Pisano, Verocchio and della Robbia to become the delight and despair of all future artists. But Mary had moved beyond the stimulus of plastic beauty, though she discussed with the Duke all these treasures as she had seen and remembered them; the works also, of the Renaissance painters

from Giotto to Raphael. And her face lit up when she told the
Duke of her delight on entering Florence, no matter from what
direction, at seeing Brunelleschi's glorious dome and the soar-
ing campanile, the marble expression of Giotto's worshipping
genius. It was part of Mary's charm that you found in her
conversation just what brought out your sympathies, so that
even her refusal of the Duke's invitation to be driven in his
carriage out to the woods at Vallombrosa was sweetened by
the pleasure with which she listened to his description of their
autumnal beauty. She never saw those woods and brooks that
Milton saw with a poet's eyes—saw and never forgot; so that
they came before him as he wrote his epic, moving him to the
unforgettable lines:

> Thick as autumnal leaves that strew the brooks
> In Vallombrosa. . . .

Robert Dudley, Duke of Northumberland, had seen them too,
and he described them tolerably well to his countrywoman, as
he chatted with her by the fire in his study on an afternoon of
wind and rain. . . .

As soon as the weather improved, Mary said her farewells.
To Robert Dudley her visit had been an interlude that was to
remain a radiant memory in his mediocre life.

Similar but shorter interludes marked Mary's passage
through Bologna and Milan. At Milan her friends would gladly
have persuaded her to postpone indefinitely her journey into
France, as her way would lie through Savoy, and because of
the war between Savoy and Spain no one had been able to
travel in that direction for two years. When they saw that she
was eager and unafraid, they let her go, but they won their
point of putting her in a carriage, where she would be more

protected than in the litter. As she passed through Vercelli, the frontier town of Piedmont, the governor of the town so marvelled when he saw her passport that he honoured her bravery by setting free an English prisoner whose anonymity prevents any biographer from becoming romantic over the incident.

Mary knew that the Nuncio at Turin would have received notice of her coming from Pope Urban. Her meeting with the Nuncio, Monsignor Caffarelli, left no doubt of the tenor of Urban's letter, for he invited her to stay at his palace, and when she was installed there he begged her to continue as his guest throughout the winter. Now, at the beginning of November, the cypresses were already weighted with snow, and the Duchess of Savoy, who gave Mary an audience at her palace, added her entreaties to the Nuncio's that Mary should remain in Turin. Again Mary was inflexible; she must go, even though it meant crossing the Alps in this inclement season. The Nuncio gave her his blessing before he sent her off in his carriage, which was to take her to the foot of Mont Cenis—a week's journey from Turin. Guides had been commissioned for the crossing of the Alps, and, with bearers and chairs, they organized the party for the crossing, joining several parties together for the sake of safety. A blinding snowstorm caught them all after a day's journey, and roads and landmarks became difficult to distinguish. The guides lost their way; four passengers perished. With great composure Mary asked the holy angels to guide them to the right road; and of course angels can make use of any of God's creatures, no matter how small. So, when a fussy little terrier belonging to one of the guides darted off from the party and looked back to suggest that they should follow, the passengers were glad to see the guides taking the hint. At length the country took on the contours the guides knew so well, and the party found itself on the French side of the Alps in the mild valley of the Rhone.

On now to Lyons where Mary stayed for one day; then to Paris. We are not surprised to learn that here she became dangerously ill, and had to spend the whole winter in that city instead of going straight on to Spa as she had arranged. As was usual on Mary's travels, friends of friends came forward in Paris, relieving her of the anxiety of establishing a household. They made her comfortable and nursed her back to health so that she was able to set out for Spa in May, 1638, going first to Liége.

Just as Mary had escaped even the smallest injury from war conditions in Savoy, so now, although the Low Countries were in a frightful state from the soldiery engaged in that part of Europe in the Thirty Years' War, she passed through with only the usual inconveniences of travel in that era. When she wrote from Liége to her cousin, Father T. Conyers, S.J., stationed as soldiers' chaplain at Dinant, telling of her safe arrival, he replied that she might esteem the success of that journey as among the chief graces God had ever given her. . . . At Liége there were no dukes or duchesses to welcome her. Ferdinand, the Prince-Bishop, was away, and the city itself had not yet got over the failure of the English Ladies, many of whom, in secular dress, were living here and there in lodgings. No one offered to give her a meal or a bed; yet this was the city where people had sung her praises not twenty years before. When those to whom she had been kind addressed words of reproach to her she spoke to them gently, so that both Winefrid and Mary Poyntz agreed in saying of her conduct: "Faults and ingratitude could never break the bond between them on her side; and what her exercise in this particular was, God only and herself could tell. At the height of all, she said with much sweetness, 'Who but I should suffer and excuse their faults?' "

In April 1618 in Liége, just twenty years before this, when making a retreat with Father Gerard, S.J., as director, she had noted: "I offered myself to suffer with love and gladness whatsoever trouble or contrariety should happen in my doing of His will. . . . I saw there was no help or comfort for me but to cleave fast to Him; and so I did, and He was there to help me." She had passed through bitter humiliation since then; had also tasted what to a weaker soul would have been the heady wine of princely esteem. But, anchored in God's love, prosperity and adversity alike found her in a tranquil mind. Whatever she had spoken to others came from her own truthful heart, and we realize something of its resources at this time when we hear her say: "We must so wholly devote ourselves to the Divine Will, that we are as it were enclosed in it; and therefore cannot on any side withdraw from it." Having lost her will in the Divine Love she was incapable of any bitterness.

When the season opened in Spa, Mary was there with her companions, who were finding it very hard to accept an arrangement (surely an oversight) of divine providence in allowing a troublesome patient to attach herself to their dear friend and Mother. This patient was suffering from cancer; and, finding inexhaustible the stores of Mary's sympathy when she met her in Liége, she followed her to Spa, allowing Mary no rest, or chance of a cure. When Winefrid and Mary Poyntz complained of this, Mary Ward replied: "As long as I do what my Master sent me for, what does it matter whether I recover or not?"[1] . . . She cared for and comforted the ailing woman, whose soul was still more ailing, as she had been away from the sacraments for many years and was averse to receiving them now, even though her disease was in an advanced state. Finally Mary's charity won her to God, and she died a happy death, almost suddenly. "The soul that loves My Truth never leaves herself any rest, but ever seeks to serve others."

In the month of May, 1639, Mary was in St. Omer on her way to England. Thirty years had passed since she had arrived there with her first seven companions. Through what a circumference of mysterious vicissitudes had her life travelled since then! Kneeling before the Blessed Sacrament in the cathedral she accepted it again in all its details in the Eternal Now of God's providence. "May the lowly homage of my service be pleasing to Thee, O most Holy Trinity. . . ."[2] In the humble silence of her heart God spoke His words of encouragement and approval, and she turned her face to England as to the last stage of her earthly pilgrimage, with the solace of the divine promise to carry her over any difficulty. And the promise with its solace was: "Be unwearied; thou art shortly to die, and thy reward shall be great." *O my God, Thou hast broken my bonds. I will sacrifice to Thee the sacrifice of praise.*

---

[1] On the subject of her death Mary used to remark in her practical way that there was no need for alarm—"it is but to pay the rent before the day."
[2] The final prayer in the Liturgy of the Mass.

19. London and Yorkshire Again

"And magic cuckoocall
Cups, clears, and olivebeo all"
(GERARD MANLEY HOPKINS)

IN APPROACHING the final years of Mary's life, we mention
again, reluctantly, that suspicious and unhappy breed of men,
the "Jerusalems." One of them in Liége originated a rumour
that Mary was being kept a prisoner at Rome and was condemned to spend the rest of her life on parole to the Inquisition. If this report were accepted in England, whither it had
travelled, it would mean a complete break between Mary and
a large group of her faithful subjects who, though in secular
dress, hoped that one day in their lifetime the Institute would
take permanent root in England. The arrival of Frances Bedingfield from Rome had steadied more than one vocation
among them, for her purposeful young life shone out of her
steady eyes as she told them about the new Roman house, and
of Pope Urban's personal interest in it. Was the Institute
really beginning all over again? "Of course," said the young
nun, surprised to think that anyone should have any fears.
Her coming among those faithful English Ladies in London
was the happiest event in their lives since the happy days before the suppression in 1631. They were heartened in their
work, and in private renewed their vows to the good God,
promising to live and work only for His love. Then came the
disturbing report that Mary Ward was kept a prisoner at

Rome. Frances was as alarmed as the others, for before she left Rome she had been given a clear picture of Mary's anxieties. As the group in London examined the report from every side, believing, doubting and again believing, the magic words were flashed to them by a friend: "Mary Ward is in London!"

In a matter of hours she was sitting in their midst, worn and obviously fighting against oncoming illness, but cheerful and affectionate. Some she was now seeing for the first time. Among these was Isabella Layton, a young convert from a wealthy Protestant home from which she had been cast on her conversion. She had then gone to the English Ladies (that was before the suppression) and asked to be accepted as a postulant and used in any way they liked, preferably as a lay-sister. When they had to disband as religious, she devoted herself to the comfort of the others, going out to beg for food when necessary, and like a serving-man, carrying home wood and provisions. In any history of the growth of the Institute in England, the name of Isabella Layton deserves a place of honour.

Mary's first visit in London was to Queen Henrietta Maria, wife of Charles I. But she had first to go through the miseries of an attack of her old malady; at the end of every journey, nature exacted this punishment from her for having driven her body with such merciless rigour. To have her with them whether sick or well was a comfort beyond description to her London companions, who cared for her and provided for her as if she were their own mother. She, for her part, cheered and encouraged all who came to her room, and shared with the seniors among them the pleasant prospect of presenting to the Queen a letter of recommendation from Cardinal Barberini, who had written it at the command of his brother, Pope Urban.

Mary had written to Urban from Liége, asking for this letter.

Finally she was out of her room and fit for the visit to the court of Charles and Henrietta. (Charles himself was in Scotland carrying out one of his ill-fated ideas of which we shall speak later.) The Queen had heard of Mary, and she received her with interest and kindness after carefully reading Cardinal Barberini's letter, in which he spoke of Mary as "much esteemed in Rome both for her well-known qualities and her piety, which will without doubt cause your Majesty willingly to see and hear her." He asks the Queen to "show all the kindness she can to her and to her company." . . . The Queen was too much worried about the growing unpopularity of her husband among his subjects to share in Mary's enthusiastic hopes for the conversion of England. This French princess, though a devout Catholic, had little hope for the English; we cannot blame her; her life in England had been lonely and unsatisfactory.

As Mary walked along the broad galleries on her way from the audience chamber, she was unaware of the nonchalant observers hanging on the walls—those bearded gentlemen and bustled ladies to whom Van Dyck's brush was giving a share in his fame. The aristocratic homes of many of them would soon be pierced by the cannon balls of Cromwell's armies, for the Parliamentary rebellion was to grow into a civil war. The latest move of Charles merely precipitated the crisis. Did he really think that the Scotch Covenanters could be forced by arms to give up their Presbyterianism for Anglicanism? If he did, he paid for his stupidity: the Civil War was to break out in 1642, and seven years later he was to lay his head on the block for the axe of the executioner.

As Mary Ward surveyed the religious and political scene

in 1639 she was often overcome by sadness to see the sectarian hatreds that divided the nation. The break with the Papacy which had taken place in her father's childhood had given England no peace. When Mary Ward returned to her country after a short absence in 1619 the Anglican ascendancy appeared as if established forever. Now, twenty years later, it looked as if the Anglicans were to be swept off the earth by the Presbyterians, goaded to ferocity by Anglican tyranny. And even that would not be the end: the break with the Papacy was to have endless reverberations. Mary could not foresee that spiritual tragedy, but her clear mind grasped the reality that the English would never be content with distorted glimpses of the Truth which their forefathers had worshipped in its fullness.

With the return of a reasonable supply of health, she at once turned to the cultivation of her own plot: the education of girls. Prepare the wives and mothers of the next generation: for thirty years this was the service she had longed to render her country. As she spoke of her ideals to her companions they felt a reawakening of their own generous impulses that they thought had been stifled forever in the years of their humiliation. Under Mary's leadership their activities became integrated: there was no squandering of energy. She gathered them all to her side and obtained the lease of a house in the neighbourhood of the French Ambassador—favouring this locality as it was only at Catholic embassies that Mass was said; and the Mass was still, as it had ever been, the centre of her life. A few days after Mary's visit to Queen Henrietta Maria she received a visit from Count Rosetti, who had arrived shortly before as Papal Nuncio to the Queen. Urban hoped that his presence would show at least to the afflicted Catholics of England that the Pope was not unmindful of them. It was a kind and gracious gesture; kind also was his action in writing special instructions to the Count to do everything in his power to assist and protect Mary Ward. Not only did he himself write to the Count, but he commanded his brother Cardinal Francesco Barberini and Donna Constanza to write in similar vein. The Count remained a constant and welcome visitor. As nuncio from a foreign power he could come quite openly, though his visits were certainly noted by pursuivants still at their old occupation of hunting out Catholics who might prefer to pay a good stiff fine rather than go to prison as recusants; the Penal Laws were still in force.

Mary's first activity on acquiring her new house was to furnish the best room for a chapel, though she and her companions lived in poverty, both as to food and clothing. On the first morning in their new residence they knelt at Mass in their beautiful little chapel, and the priest left the Blessed Sacrament in the tabernacle. If Mary was not in her room attending to business you would find her in the chapel, her grateful heart answering by her presence the plaint of our Lord: "Could you not watch one hour with me?" Like many holy persons who have done great work for God she was a contemplative whose love overflowed in work for souls. We have only a few notes of her spiritual life; but we may perhaps reverently gauge something of the depth of her union with God when we read a note made at a retreat in spiritual solitude in Liége nearly thirty years before. It shows the trend of her prayer in those early years. After saying that she had a sudden and clear realization of God's indwelling in her soul, she noted: "I endeavoured to go forward according to the points of meditation, but could not. He held my heart; I could not work. I would then have asked Him something and bid Him welcome; but He would not let me. . . . I saw plainly that His only will was that I should neither work nor talk, but hold my peace in all." Comparing that brief note with the teaching of St. Teresa, we feel that she and Mary are companions along the privileged ways of mystical prayer.

Word quickly passed among priests in hiding in London that one could say Mass at Mary Ward's house and could go in at any time to take from the tabernacle the Blessed Sacrament. These priests risked their lives every time they went out ministering to souls. Of course they wore the ordinary dress of the period and often went under assumed names. As they turned into the house used by the English Ladies they might have been any social visitors; especially was this so when Mary was entrusted by many Catholic parents with the care of their young daughters. As we think of all the Catholic friendliness surrounding Mary during these years in London we wonder whether all the threatened enmity had evaporated, or whether it ever had existed except among a small minority whose personal troubles had made them abnormally suspicious. We hear no more of any "Jerusalems." As many as five priests at a time made the house their headquarters, and were braver and more devoted to Our Lord because of the intrepid woman who encouraged them on every arduous enterprise. One or other of them would occasionally remind Mary with a smile that her hospitality and her chapel were an open invitation to pursuivants; but Mary would laugh and say that they were among her early childhood memories, and that for the sake of old times she would like to practise again the clever methods of escape that were part of her girlhood education; and a flash of the old Yorkshire spirit could be seen in her smile.

One night, while Mary was praying in the chapel before going to bed, there was the sound of heavy boots on the front porch and a knock at the door. Two of Mary's companions were with her; they guessed at once that it was a visit by pursuivants, but there was no panic—the situation had often been discussed. They went at once to the altar to ensure that the Blessed Sacrament should be out of danger by lifting the tabernacle into a secret panel in the wall. The blows of pikes were now on the door: "Open, in the King's name!" By this time everyone in the house was up and dressed. Mary sent an urgent message to three priests who occupied one wing to leave at once. She then went herself and opened the door. She gently asked the pursuivants why her household was being disturbed at that hour of the night. They seemed shamefaced in her presence, but the leader spoke up to state their business, and Mary stood back with dignity to let them pass. They found nothing out of which they could make a case, and left; but Mary, who, like many of God's servants, had through faith recovered strength from weakness, sat up all night, after insisting that the schoolgirls return to their beds. At intervals of a few hours all next day the pursuivants returned, so that they paid four visits in all during twenty-four hours. They lifted carpets, ripped up mattresses, and tapped viciously round the wainscot of every room. A phenomenon noted by Mary's companions was that they left her room untouched; if a pursuivant happened to enter there he would leave hurriedly, humbly asking pardon for having come in. "And this not once, but always, whether the searchers were pursuivants or soldiers."

The next day the children—about twenty of them—found it very hard to settle to their lessons; and because of the disturbance they were given extra recreation. All kinds of stories came to light then—grandfathers' tales, and many versions of the worst pursuivant raid ever. They declaimed and giggled, though their eloquence faded noticeably when their teacher, Winefrid Wigmore, said: "Now, we'll say all that in Italian . . . or French . . . or German." This was no nursery school; mental and cultural work occupied the day, which began every morning with Mass. As Mary saw the brown and blonde and black heads through their white veils in the chapel, she thanked God for allowing her to work (old and ill as she often felt) at this ideal that had called to her young womanhood over thirty years before. In the early days of the Institute she had written in her private note-book: "When any lights or other motions occur to me about the Institute I shall commend the same unto the Sacred Wounds of Christ, and make acts of resignation." As she looked, over the well-brushed heads in their net veils, to the altar where the priest was lifting up the Sacred Host at Mass, her spirit hid in the wounds of Our Lord as she asked Him to take her life completely into His so that it might become wholly divinized. Every day her soul thirsted more and more to promote God's glory, and her whole day had become a sacrifice for that glory that mortals can procure by living hidden with Christ in God: *Per ipsum et cum ipso et in ipso.*[1] As she said the words in her heart with the priest, all her ideals and desires focussed in that sublime prayer. She did not have the distraction that we, looking back on the scene, are permitted as we survey the girlish heads: this is the only Catholic school in England, and if its existence as a school were known, Mary could be put in prison. . . . The word "school" was never mentioned.

1 "Through Him, and with Him, and in Him. . . ."

The parents of these girls were influential Catholics, and they were so delighted with the progress and contentment of their daughters under the care of Mary Ward that they spoke of her among their Protestant friends at court, where Anglicans and Catholics were drawing together as the Puritans, who hated both, were rising to power. Court ladies visited Mary, at first from curiosity; those who came again and again found in her company the courage to face the storm that was to sweep away the court of Charles I and his wife. Among the Catholic visitors it soon became known that Mary Ward corresponded with Pope Urban, and it was to her that these English people turned if they had need of asking any favour of the Papacy.

Mary in her letters to Urban gave him a picture of Catholic life in London, but she said too:

How much greater consolation would it be to me to find myself now at your sacred feet, than here in my own country among my relations! A severe illness of nearly three months, which still oppresses me, prevented me, much against my wish, from leaving this in the autumn. But in spring, ill or well, if God gives me life, I shall not fail to set off on my journey to Rome, where the presence and protection of my supreme Father and exalted Patron will make me truly happy. And one day, at those sacred feet, I trust some grace may be granted to me, which until now my sins have not made me worthy to obtain. Nevertheless, I will never abuse such great kindness by importuning for anything which does or might displease you. Most humbly entreating pardon for my present boldness, prostrate I kiss the sacred feet of your Holiness.

London, February 14, 1641.

Maria della Guardia

But Mary Ward had said her last good-bye to Rome. Within a few months of the writing of this letter, it was made impossible for any private individual to leave England, and early in 1642 the Civil War broke over the country, which was rent between the two parties, Royalists and Roundheads (as the Parliamentarians with their shaven heads were called). Charles I went northwards, followed by all the Royalists who could leave London; the city was no longer a place where Mary with her noted household could live in safety, so on May 1st the whole household packed themselves with their belongings into three large coaches and set out for Yorkshire. A priest went with them as chaplain, and of course Robert Wright was also in attendance. It was only when they all found themselves safely launched on their journey in the quiet countryside north of London that they realized how fortunate they were in escaping from the city, where spies and pursuivants were inspecting every party that travelled on its outgoing thoroughfares. Mary's impressive exit from London was not as foolhardy as we might at first judge it to be: she had learnt from her early encounters with spies and informers in England that it was often safer to put on a bold front and to travel with display of importance which kept those minions at a distance. So, out in the countryside, lovely with springtime freshness, the children sang and enjoyed themselves as their coaches bumped and rattled along. When they came to the uplands and were let out for lunch and a run along the lanes, flowers and young hedges in bud welcomed them and they heard the cuckoo calling his name to the listening hills. Mary and her companions thought with a twist of sadness in their hearts of the stories their parents used to tell them of the May Day processions and the crowning of the Queen of Heaven in those happy days when England was known as Mary's Dowry. As Mary sat resting on a bank in the warm sunshine her heart gathered up the beauty of all the lovely sights and sounds and perfumes in silent worship. Then, turning to the psalms that had nourished her piety since childhood, she said half to herself: *Omnis terra adoret te, Deus, et psallat tibi.*[2]

The children climbed into the coaches again; the whole party was reseated, and the horses plunged forward to the sound of the cracking whips. Tonight they would sleep at a village; then, on again, each day a little bit longer than the foregoing one—at least, that is how it seemed to the girls, who were growing tired. Towards the end, their enthusiasm revived when Mary told them that they were going to be guests at homes where she had lived as a girl in Yorkshire.

That was indeed an interesting prospect for these girls; it is so difficult for schoolgirls to picture a revered mistress enjoying the delights of youth. The girls watched as men and women greeted her as if she were a long-lost sister. At Ripley Castle, Sir William Ingleby, lately made a baronet by Charles, came forward as host to his much-travelled cousin: Mary and he had played together fifty years before. Reunions of equal warmth took place at Studley Royal, where another cousin, Sir John Mallory, was the host. She spent a week or so at each of these homes, enjoying walks by the rivers and in the woods enriched with countless childhood memories.

At Babthorpe courteous strangers welcomed Mary. They were not Catholics, and perhaps felt a little embarrassed to meet this Englishwoman broken in health by journeys and sufferings in foreign lands where she had gone to live because she could not live without her Catholic faith. Her relationship with the Babthorpes gave an additional touch of discomfiture, for Sir Ralph Babthorpe had lost his beautiful home to the

2 "Let all the earth adore Thee, O God, and sing a hymn to Thee."

present owners, who had considered that Babthorpe Hall and its surrounding estates were worth more than their loyalty to God. When Mary saw their hunting trophies in the room that had been the chapel, she nearly broke down. She went no further after that, but took leave of her hostess in her own graceful manner, trying not to think of her dear Barbara Babthorpe, now far away in Rome, she, too, an exile because of her faith.

At Newby Hall a special pleasure awaited her: the welcome of a group of old servants who had served her parents in her childhood years. They crowded round her now, their furrowed, weather-beaten faces looking beautiful, so Mary thought, in their delighted excitement. She spoke with each one separately, and they brought out of their treasure boxes, crudely fashioned little objects (needle-cases, rosary bags and purses) that Mary had worked for them in those laborious days of needlecraft, when knots were so ubiquitous. After a short stay in the friendliness and sympathy of that environment, Mary was on her way again; she had not come to Yorkshire to linger over memories. She must find somewhere to live with her large household.

On the feast of the Holy Cross, the 14th of September, 1642, they made an end of their travels at the old mansion of Hutton Rudby, belonging to Sir Thomas Gascoigne, one of Mary's many cousins. Amid wild, secluded woods, it was visited only by those on pilgrimage to the shrine at the old Carthusian monastery of Mount Grace. The only residents in that wild bit of Yorkshire were poor farmers, most of them Catholics. The delight of these good folk was unbounded when they heard that a Catholic household had taken over Hutton Rudby, where there was now a chapel and a priest to say Mass. It sounded too heavenly to be true, and a few hesitant visits were necessary before they could be convinced. Those who were thorough enough in their investigations were rewarded by a meeting with the lady of the house. No elegant converse in French or Italian or German had been able to destroy completely the homely music of her Yorkshire accent, and she welcomed her new neighbours as people who belonged to her: this was her, and their, little corner of England.

On the other side of the county battles were being fought between the Royalists and the Parliamentarians as the Civil War worked up to carnage. Soon there was word of raids by small parties of anti-Royalist troops in the vicinity of Hutton Rudby. Then one Saturday afternoon a breathless messenger from the village arrived to say that a captain and forty of his troops were to make a raid on Mary's house. Mary calmly called the household to prayers to await the attack; but evening fell and no horsemen appeared to break the purple skyline of the moors. At about eight o'clock a solitary soldier called to ask for some oats for his horse. The whole household, except Mary who was very ill, sat up all night; and with the sunrise came the captain of the troop, to demand that he be shown the trunks of gold and armour that were reported to be hidden in the house. The portress courteously denied the charge but allowed him to enter for the search. The captain made little show of searching, and soon bowed himself out the hall-door; for which mercy he was given twenty shillings. In a few moments he rode back and held out the twenty shillings to the portress, saying that his soldiers would only spend them on drink. Winefrid Wigmore, who accompanied the portress throughout the happenings, did not doubt that their pleasant issue was due wholly to Mary Ward, whose "humble, peaceful confidence and cheerfulness" brought God's protection round them. After recovering from her bout of sickness Mary set up in the household special devotions to the nine choirs of angels, as her plan of defence against further military visits.

Mary had one persistent worry at this time: the absence of news from Rome, and even from the few companions she had left behind in London two years before. Though the obscure setting of Hutton Rudby was safer than any district nearer York, the absence of any sure transmission of letters was a great source of anxiety. Two years, and not a line from London or Rome! She could endure that famine no longer. Another house was found at Hewarth, about a mile outside the walled city of York, which at this time was almost overflowing with Royalist families intent on refuge after the mounting successes of the Parliamentarian troops. The refugees were merely inviting a siege.

Out in their new home at Hewarth, Mary and her companions established the ordered routine of prayer and work which was their life. Mass was said every morning in the small chapel where the Blessed Sacrament was reserved. Two priests made it their headquarters for their apostolate in the country places around and behind Hewarth; and every priest who passed that way was sure of a warm welcome and hospitality. As soon as the Royalist families in York heard of Mary's household they came out in numbers to visit her. Mary gave the young sisters[3] talks on their duties in these social contacts, giving them as an ideal: "I will fly all manner of esteem and yet carry myself so that I may be grateful[4] to all." . . . By April, 1644, the pleasant social visits were becoming rare as the Parlia-

3 Frances Bedingfield was one of these.
4 "Pleasing."

mentarian troops advanced on York. On the 3rd of June the siege began in good earnest, with Oliver Cromwell as one of the leaders. The Hewarth household, at the earnest behest of their friends in York, moved into the city, where for the six weeks of the siege they shared the strain and sufferings of the citizens of the beleaguered fortress. When the city yielded, the garrison of York and any citizens who wished were allowed to retire to some other of the King's fortresses, this being the terms of the surrender. On hearing that none of the other royal fortresses promised much in the way of safety, Mary decided to return with her household to Hewarth. In their absence four hundred soldiers had been lodged in the house, and gardens and buildings were in a horrible state of destruction. There were two rooms that escaped the general inroads of dirt and vandalism: they were the room that had been used as the chapel and Mary's own room, both of which were left untouched, even to the mats on the floors. The sisters, with awe in their hearts, recalled that Mary had asked St. Michael to take one end of the village and St. Joseph the other end, in their special care. They wryly attributed the rest of the shambles to their own want of confidence in the heavenly hosts.

20. Mary's Last Word

*"This hath ever been a comfort to me: that
I chose Jesus for my Heaven."*

(DAME JULIAN OF NORWICH)

THE POOR food and the bad air that were only two of the disadvantages of living in the besieged city of York played havoc
with Mary's feeble health; nor was it improved by her solicitude for all who came to her in those weeks for comfort and
advice. When she returned to Hewarth she was a dying woman
with less than six months to live; and so very tired that she
said one day with a smile to Mary Poyntz: "I have much to
do not to beg Our Lord to take me." The Parliamentarians
were keeping such a close watch on Catholic homes that no
priest could say Mass for Mary's household for three months.
This privation, and the absence of the Blessed Sacrament, was
the chief grief of Mary's heart during the closing months of her
life. Another grief, though not so piercing, was the continued
absence of letters. At last dear Winefrid Wigmore put a few
belongings together and with a lay-sister set out to walk to London to bring home news for her dying friend. That heroic act
of friendship should be mentioned wherever great deeds of
friendship are discussed. While Winefrid was on her journey,
Mary would say each day what stage of the journey had been
reached, even to saying with accuracy on such a day "she will
be home in time to help to bury me."[1] Mary often spoke of her

[1] Winefrid returned without letters, eight days before Mary's death.

208

death to her companions and tried to make them take a cheerful view of it; so set was she against sadness that they took good care to bathe their tear-reddened eyes before they went into her room.

Christmas brought the joy of a visit from a priest who said Midnight Mass and risked his life by staying in the house for the Christmas Octave to say Mass every morning. Mary was present at each Mass, and who could measure the degree of her adoring love and gratitude?

On the Feast of St. Thomas of Canterbury towards evening she felt a deadly cold and sharp pains over her whole body. She said to her companions, "This is something more than ordinary. I will go and offer myself to our dear Lord in the chapel." Before the Blessed Sacrament she remained half an hour in prayer and then went to her bed, to leave it no more. On New Year's Day, 1645, she made a general confession and received what she alone realized was her last Communion. The priest had to leave very early next morning, and Mary implored him to anoint her before he departed. He could not believe her so ill, and she would not urge him to stay at his own great peril, but when he was gone she said quietly, "Patience! I must not have that happiness, for I know well there will be no means hereafter."

To Mary Poyntz she said "That nothing may be wanting to my pains, I do not only not make my daily Communions, but I have not even the satisfaction of thinking that I feel the want of that great grace—as if I did not esteem it as I have done."

Mary Poyntz, in a letter to Barbara Babthorpe, tells something of those last weeks, speaking of Mary with the concealment which cannot have concealed much, as "our dearest my father" and calling the members of the household by male names.

"I would ask sometimes where his pain was; he answered 'from head to foot' . . . yet never changed his sweet, serene look, as it were between jest and earnest. Ned said 'If you die, we will take pack in lap and away to the heathen.' He answered: 'If I thought so, it would break my heart.' . . . Will begged he would ask of God his own life . . . asked if he had done it, he answered: 'Yes, entirely and most resignedly.' . . . Then commended to us with greatest feeling the practice of God's vocation in us . . . constantly, efficaciously and affectionately . . . said 'God will assist you and help you, it is no matter the who but the what; and when God,' said he, 'shall enable me to be in place I will serve you.' Then with greatest love embracing each seemed to mind us no more but with eyes and hands gave expression of sweet intrinsical [interior], entire acts. . . ."

Whatever her spiritual darkness and physical anguish Mary was ready always to cheer the others. The memory would ever remain with them of a mortal who even in this life had eluded for ever the shade of sadness. But as sorrow held them Mary said "O fie fie! what, still look sad! Come, let us rather sing and praise God joyfully for His infinite loving-kindness."

She began to sing, and her companions joined her with broken voices, some hymn of praise and thanksgiving they had been wont to sing together. Mary sang on till she had no breath left. Twenty-four hours later she was dead. Her last words were "Jesus, Jesus, Jesus."

21. After Mary's Death

*"When God shall enable me to be in place
I will serve you."*

(MARY WARD)

THE MORNING after Mary's death, the priest, who had been trying to reach the house for some weeks, arrived at Hewarth. As
he looked down at her face, peaceful with the majesty of death,
he marvelled at the ways of God with a soul whose whole life
had been devoted to the diffusion of His Eucharistic Love: she
had to cross the threshold of death without the Holy Bread to
sustain her. But God's peace filled the house. How should it
not be so after the flight of a soul who had been true to the
ideal of "living wholly unto God in Christ Jesus, Our Lord"?
In early childhood, all unknown to her baby intelligence, her
lips had spoken her love when they spoke their first word,
"Jesus," sealing with a smile an allegiance that was to last a
lifetime. Later on, the smile had often to conquer tears, but the
love remained shining bright, giving light to all whose lives
were linked with hers.

Mary's body was buried in the only available burial ground
—the churchyard of the Protestant church in the village of
Osbaldwick, a mile or so from Hewarth. Nothing now remains to show she was buried there but the gravestone leaning
against the porch, telling us that she loved the poor and that
she was sixty years of age in January 1645. Her body was taken
away (at some period of the Cromwellian regime probably),
but whether by friend or foe no one now knows.

Towards the end of 1649 the owners of the house at Hewarth notified the Superior, Mary Poyntz, that it must be vacated. Cromwell set up his government that year after the execution of Charles I, and the plight of Catholics became as tragic as at any period in history. Hewarth, or any village in England, was no longer a place for Mary Ward's companions; so it was with great joy that Mary Poyntz accepted the offer of a sum of money from her cousin, the Marquess of Worcester. The way was now clear to go to Paris, where Mary Ward had made friends during the few months she spent there on her way home from Rome in 1638. A number of those hardy little pupils who had been with them at Hewarth went with them, some of them entering with them as postulants. Mary Poyntz remained as Superior for two years, until Barbara Babthorpe, the Superior General in Rome, called her to come to her because of Barbara's ill-health. Mary Poyntz travelled by way of Munich and on arrival in Rome was elected Superior General.

Knowing that Mary Ward desired the propagation of the Institute, even though it was not yet confirmed, Mary Poyntz accepted the invitation of the Prince-Elector of Bavaria to found a house in Augsburg. By 1666 the house was not only flourishing but was under the protection of the Prince-Bishop of that city. He publicly declared them religious, settled a yearly revenue for them, and appointed priests to say Mass in their chapel. The way was thus paved for the Confirmation of the Rules of the Institute, which took place on June 13, 1703.

But to return to England: in 1669 Frances Bedingfield left Paris for her own country. Within the walled city of York a house was given to her and her companions by Mary Ward's cousin, Sir Thomas Gascoigne. Thus was founded the Bar

Convent, which soon became a renowned school for girls under the personal interest of Queen Beatrice, the wife of Charles II. At the time of writing this biography, the Bar Convent continues its good work, holding to its traditions and preserving the spirit of Mary Ward even while it holds its place among the foremost convent schools in England, where it was the first to be founded after the Reformation.

During the eighteenth century the Institute of the Blessed Virgin Mary, as it was officially called after Pope Clement XI confirmed its Rules in 1703, flourished in dozens of convents in Germany and Italy, conditions of princely favour in Bavaria providing the beautiful convent of Nymphenburg which became the head house. But the Napoleonic Wars cut across all their communications and the various houses had to fend for themselves. It is only in this century that they have drawn together again under a Generalate in Rome.

A branch of the Institute was founded in Dublin by Mother Mary Teresa Ball, a gifted and holy woman whom Archbishop Murray encouraged to make her novitiate in the Bar Convent, York, so that the Institute might open a convent in Dublin. In 1821, Reverend Mother Teresa Ball made the foundation, calling the house Loreto, after the Holy House in Italy, beloved by Mary Ward. The house at Rathfarnham, Dublin, thus came to be called Loreto Abbey, and its numerous affiliations have kept the name, Loreto.

In 1847 Rathfarnham made its first foundation in Canada, which has since grown into a flourishing Generalate with its head house in Toronto, ruling several important centres, chiefly at Niagara Falls and over the border in Chicago. When the Canadian foundation was made it was the custom for each foundation to become autonomous. As Toronto did not seek affiliation with Rathfarnham (Australia, on the other hand, did seek it), it became and remains a Generalate separate from Rathfarnham, to which, however, it is bound by ties of a common Rule and sisterly affection, and—the bond that binds the whole Institute together—a devotion to Mother Mary Ward and a strong desire for her beatification.

Epilogue by *Maisie Ward*

I FEARED to spoil the enjoyment of Mother Oliver's swift and exciting narrative by putting into the Introduction a discussion of the events of those crucial years of Mary's life 1621–1631.

The researches of the two Fathers Grisar—the author of the well-known book on Martin Luther and his nephew—those of Mother Mary Salome and the masterly reconstruction by Father Leo Hicks, S.J.,[1] add a good deal to what was known when Mother Chambers wrote her biography. Unfortunately there are still gaps: some of Mary's letters were destroyed and a whole box of documents was lost in a shipwreck. An outline can now be made with some degree of confidence, but it leaves many problems as to the hows and whys of this fascinating story. I have attempted in this brief epilogue to pursue a little further the historical problems which could not have been discussed by Mother Oliver without spoiling the flow of her narrative. Of necessity in so doing I go over a little of the ground already covered in her narrative, as otherwise the train of events would not be clear.

Had Father Lee lived on or Father Gerard remained at hand, Mary might even have achieved the impossible and won confirmation of her Institute. No one studying them closely can fail to be amazed at the contrast in tone between the first memorial to Paul V and the later one to Gregory XV. Yet I feel

[1] In *The Month* 1928–29: six articles.

convinced Mary did not herself realize this difference. She was as utterly submissive at the later as at the earlier date—yet the later letter is so blunt as to be startling. She could have again outlined the Rule so admirably described in her first appeal by which the Institute had now been living *with papal authority* for twelve years. But she did not even remind the new Pope of his predecessor's approval. She need not—as in the earlier paper she did not—bring in the name of the Jesuits. But in this she gave the papal approval of their order as a chief reason for the approval of her own. Probably by Father Lee's advice she had asked for theological opinions, and one or two of these were heavily in her favour. In this memorial they are not mentioned. Perhaps she thought copies were already in the Vatican archives, but it is never safe to assume that a search will be made for documents of whose existence the judge may not be aware. But above all, any wise counsellor would have warned Mary not to open her memorial with the statement that "by Divine appointment" she and hers wanted to take this Rule—for this was the very question under consideration.

Mary's English biographer, Mother Chambers, though seeing how unfortunate this memorial was, seems almost proud of the fact that it proved Mary "a true Englishwoman." Belonging to that race myself, I feel it one of our great misfortunes that we are too liable to speak bluntly, hence quite unconsciously alienating people of good will. In Mary's case it was only on paper, for in conversation she won all hearts. . . . And by a sad irony her immense attractiveness was the second cause of her undoing.

She could not be everywhere at once, yet the Institute was in demand on all sides: at once a tribute to her and a confession that a vital need existed which it alone was filling. Day-schools

for girls, free schools for the poor. Rulers and bishops in the
Low Countries, in Germany, in Italy, in Hungary, were entreating her on all hands to open these schools in their cities.
And Mary could not bear to refuse. Her letters are full of
contrivances, by moving one nun here and sending another
there, to stretch her scanty resources in numbers, by sending
a few gold pieces from one house to another (sometimes lost
in transit), to stretch her even scantier resources in coin of any
realm. Dowries were not coming from England, rulers promised support and forgot to supply it. And alas, some also
forgot to get permission from the local bishop before the
lightning opening of a convent without which their realm
would be desolate. In short, Mary was the fashion.

Father Gerard had seen it all, and he wrote in 1627 to the
younger Father Lee (nephew of Mary's first friend), begging
him to persuade Mary to rest her case on the good running
of the Munich house. "Choice persons," he said, should be
"placed in that house, and better were it to have that house
well and fully furnished, than to strive and strain to erect
others though they were offered even by the Emperor." Admirers of their success should be left longing for them, "companions of the best sort" would join them from every country.
At present "fear of entering" resulted from the Institute's remaining unconfirmed, especially in England where it was
"much bruited that they shall never be confirmed, but rather
suppressed." His conclusion was "to undertake few places, but
there to discharge well."

When Mary reached Rome in October 1621 Gregory XV
"received her with singular benevolence and all fatherly and
benign expressions, so far as to say 'God had in good time pro-

vided for His Church,' alluding to the profit that was to come from her labours." He put the examination of the Institute into the hands of the Congregation of Bishops and Regulars. And Mary's enemies were prompt to pour into their ears the stories against it, "the Ladies preach in pulpits," "they are much talked about for petulance and undecorum," etc. Mr. Bennett (the secular clergy were not then called Father) was supplied with a letter signed by the leading clergy of England, and Kellison of Douai joined in the attack.

Two years later Pope Gregory died and Urban VIII, elected Pope, received Mary at Frascati. Again came the papal blessing that apparently did so little to influence the canon lawyers. Urban, like Gregory, was more than fatherly. He gave Mary permission for a chapel in the house. He agreed to her request for a smaller commission to examine her case and put on it men he thought would be favourable. Meanwhile, in the same year the new Congregation of Propaganda had been set up, by which the affairs of missionary countries were to be handled. England was now a missionary country, and the new agent of the English Clergy (Mr. Rant was his somewhat appropriate name) lost no time in getting in touch with the secretary of Propaganda. This man, Dr. Francis Ingoli, appears, says Father Hicks, "to have been a convinced and somewhat blustering bureaucrat." Already a hater of Jesuits, he wrote on the back of a letter "Jesuitissarum institutum examinatur ut prohibeatur." "Examined in order to be condemned": faced by such an attitude, what hope had it?

Curiously enough, the first move made was to close in 1625 the school at Rome—to the bitter grief of the parents. But *at the same time* the Pope endowed the Institute with a pension. Father Hicks suggests that the closing of the school was "a

mere expedient to allay the opposition," by withdrawing the
Ladies from public notice.

In 1628 the four cardinals declared the Institute "contrary
to the sacred canons." There should be no further extension—
with a view to future suppression. Later in the same year this
was confirmed by Propaganda, and letters were sent to the
Nuncios at Brussels and Naples ordering the closing of the
convents in their area. The local Nuncios, more aware of the
vast good the Institute was effecting, and sensitive to the admiration and love it had won among rulers and people, hesitated
and argued. Mary had left Rome, since her other houses needed
her, when it had become certain that there would anyhow be
no quick confirmation: the Brussels Nuncio, Pallotto, urged
her to return there, but without telling her what had happened.
So in 1629 Mary was once more pleading before Pope Urban,
unaware of the *Fiat* that had already gone forth from Propaganda. And, so reluctant were the local cardinals and Nuncios
to act, that two years after the decree Ingoli had only succeeded in getting Naples and Flanders to carry it out. And the
Pope *the year after it had been issued* granted Mary's request
to have the Institute once more discussed by a small commission of four cardinals. There seems no possible reason for this
except a hope on his part to be able to withdraw the decree
should the cardinals report favourably. Not only did Mary
write a long memorial for them, but she was allowed *contrary
to all precedent* to plead before the cardinals in person, speaking for nearly an hour.

Father Hicks believes that Mary had been kept by her
enemies from any knowledge of the decree of Propaganda
from their fear that if she knew of it she would persuade the
Pope to rescind it, and also from the hope that *not* knowing of

it she would in some way compromise herself. In this they were successful, for Mary, hearing for the first time that houses were being closed and convinced that this was without the Pope's knowledge or consent, wrote a letter to Liége (perhaps meant for the other houses also), telling them to disregard the decree and to explain with modesty and respect their reasons for doing so. Even if, as was unlikely, bishops and Nuncios should excommunicate them, let them suffer it. A remedy would soon present itself.

Mary wrote, we are told, *tempestive*—and equally *tempestive* withdrew her orders on learning that the Pope had in fact signed the decree of Propaganda. But her letter—or rather a copy of it—got into the hands of the one Nuncio unfavourable to her, who forwarded it to Ingoli. Here was matter for proceedings that would force the hands of Mary's reluctant friends, and seal her doom. Ingoli handed the document over to the Holy Office.

Of course if Mary left Rome in 1629, as her biographies state, this letter would not be genuine, but it seems more propable that she left in 1630. The letter is generally accepted as hers. What has puzzled the researchers is the question of Mary's attitude and that of Winefrid Wigmore sent by her to several convents *after* she knew the Propaganda decree had papal approval. Her enemies claimed that she had through Winefrid resisted its execution. But, as Father Hicks so well shows, it had in fact been carried out to the letter, only the letter was not as devastating as her enemies claimed and desired. Schools were shut, bells ceased to ring, religious titles were no longer used—but the ladies still lived in community, for this had *not* been forbidden, and still continued to pray together.

But for many years after the Holy Office had acted, Mary and her Institute worked on only in virtue of the Pope's personal permission. The documents stored in the Archives had all been arranged and interpreted by the enemy so that when in 1703 Clement XI confirmed the Institute the nuns were forbidden to call Mary their Foundress. It was Pius X who solemnly lifted this ban, while Pius XI on the tercentenary of the Munich convent paid high tribute to her.

The most startling thing about Ingoli's attitude—and indeed of all those instrumental in wrecking the Institute—was the readiness with which they received insubstantial rumours *against* it and their indifference to the enormous value of it repeatedly urged by those who had seen it in action.

Nuncios and bishops wrote pressingly of the bitter need for these schools, especially in heretical countries. With Mary's perished a half dozen that had been opened by groups of lay women on similar lines. In vain their ordinaries pleaded that they were no part of the English Ladies Institute. Ingoli mowed them down, and although Secretary of Propaganda he suggested no alternative way of propagating the Faith in those desolate lands where these women were striving to keep it alive.

The story is vividly told by Mother Oliver of Mary's second visit to Rome; of her pleading before the cardinals, of her return to Munich, the suppression of the Institute and Mary's own imprisonment in the convent of the Anger as "heretic, schismatic and rebel to Holy Church"; of her letters from prison, written in lemon juice, of her appeal to the Pope, and the Pope's anger when he heard of Mary's imprisonment; of his instant order for her release.

With his permission Mary, as we have seen, opened a school in Rome. The Institute had been dissolved, its members scattered, but gathering the fragments she began again, not afraid of being under the Pope's eyes, but rather courting his close attention to her work.

And then, shattered in health though she was, unable often to move from place to place, except in a litter into which she must be lifted, in pain from head to foot, she set out once more for England. "My meaning is," she calmly wrote, "to endeavour by prayer and private negotiation that we may have common schools in the great city of London, which will never be without a miracle."

Down to the end Mary's letters seem those of a young woman ready to begin her work, not of one old and ill whose course was almost run. She was in fact committing it on earth to her children, leaving them and the work confidently to God. When one of them said, "If you die we will take pack in lap and away to the heathen," Mary answered, "If I thought so it would break my heart." They must not depend on her but on "God's vocation in us." She said, "God will assist and help you, it is no matter the who but the what; and when God shall enable me to be in place I will serve you."

Already she had served her country and the Church at the cost of much toil and suffering. The story is told dramatically and enthusiastically by Mother Oliver. But there is something still to be done by those of us whom Mary has served as individuals, whether as nuns in her order or as pupils in her schools. Let us pray ardently that this "incomparable" woman may be canonized in our generation.

Appendix I

A. *Plight of the Poor after the Reformation in England*

In his novel, *Sybil*, Disraeli, looking back over the three hundred years that divided him from the days of the Suppression of the Monasteries by Henry VIII, writes (speaking through one of his characters): "All agree that the monastics were easy landlords; their rents were low; they granted leases in those days. Their tenants too might renew their term before their tenure ran out; so they were men of spirit and property. There were yeomen then, Sir; the country was not divided into two classes, masters and slaves; there was some resting-place between luxury and misery." Disraeli's point is one of contrast with his own era of nineteenth-century England.

B. *Secret Hiding-Places for Priests*

The country mansions in Tudor England were suitable for making hiding-places. They had thick walls and enormous chimney-stacks and a great deal of oak panelling. But the work had to done at dead of night.

Nicholas Owen, a carpenter by trade, and later, a Jesuit lay-brother, was well-known as a builder of hiding-places. He would construct them in all sorts of unexpected corners: among the flues of great chimney-stacks, between a false floor and the ceiling of the room below, in the solid walls behind the panelling, down among the sewers or up

223

in the roof. Sometimes he would have one hiding-place beyond another, and even a third beyond that; and he nearly
always contrived to have at least two and sometimes three
entrances to each hide, whether under a window-seat or a
hearth-stone.

In the autoboigraphy of Father John Gerard, S.J., there
is a good deal about Nicholas Owen and his marvellous
hiding-places. When Father Gerard escaped from the
Tower of London in 1597, it was Owen who organized the
escape. He was closely connected with nearly all Father
Gerard's adventures in England, and there was scarcely a
country home he visited that did not have a system of
hiding-places constructed by Owen. Brave Nicholas
Owen! In 1605 he died a martyr's death after being tortured.

Appendix II: Education in Mary Ward's Schools

PROFESSOR GUILDAY tells us that the school of the Institute of the Blessed Virgin Mary opened at St. Omer was the first free school for English Catholic girls governed by women living in community. We may mention here that wherever Mary founded a boarding-school, she also opened a free school for those who wished to attend.

The times being what they were, the chief stress in her educational programme was on the training of character. From a page of the Diocesan Archives of Augsburg, now in the Archives of the Institute at Altoetting, we read, "The girls are to be trained in self-discipline, to realize their duties towards God, their neighbour and themselves, and to adore God in spirit and in truth." They were to be trained "to be good and capable mistresses of a house, and gentle, peace-loving and cheerful members of society."

The school curriculum allowed generous time to the study of languages, both classic and modern. Mary herself was an accomplished linguist, and Winefrid Wigmore could write and converse in five languages. This bent towards languages so evident in Mary Ward's schools was strengthened by the circumstances in which her Institute developed, causing an interchange of teaching nuns between their various houses, whether in German-speaking countries, in Italy or in France. The transference of nuns from one country to another meant that there were multi-lingual teachers in the schools, for one of the Rules of the Institute was, and still is, that "all must learn the language of the country they live in." No matter how far away Mary was she liked to follow the progress of studies in the schools. In 1627 she wrote to the Mistress of Schools in Munich: "This is chiefly to congratulate you on the unexpected progress of your Latin schools. You cannot easily believe the content I took in the themes of those two girls. You will work much to your happiness by advancing them apace in that learning and God will concur with you because His honour and service so require: no talent is to be so much regarded in them as the Latin tongue." There follows a touch of humour: "I fear these subtle wenches have some help at home to make their themes; but you will look to them for that." These girls would have been pupils at the secondary day-school in Munich. Mary was the pioneer of such schools in Germany, where her boarding-, secondary-, day- and free primary schools flourished until the secularization under Napoleon.

She would allow only trained teachers in her schools; and the excellence of their qualifications may be gauged by a sentence from the State Archives at Mainz. The reference is to schools in the eighteenth century and reads thus: "The Institute B.V.M. is the most successful in the turning out of teachers, because the nuns are trained precisely with that object in view during their noviceship." At the end of the eighteenth century the training of secular teachers was to the fore in Germany. Inspectors were sent to the convents of the I.B.V.M.; and a sentence from the report of the Chief Inspector may be quoted: "The methods of these ladies opened my eyes and made me wish to have similar work done by the State."

To return to the first half of the seventeenth century when Mary Ward was establishing her schools; it is interesting to take a closer look at the school curriculum, which covered all the intellectual and cultural interests of the era. Natural sciences and mathematics were an unexplored field, the keeping of household accounts being all that was required of an educated lady of the day in the realm of figures.

But intellectually the judgment was trained by the scope given to dialectic in the class-room, and by disputations, where the class was divided into two camps, made ready thinkers and clear speakers as each girl stood up to defend her thesis. Subjects in philosophy or incidents taken from their studies in the classics and modern languages—all these provided theses for disputations.

The lighter side of the curriculum in Mary's schools covered drama, music, dancing, drawing and painting. The acting of plays, dramatized from scriptural or secular reading, was considered as important in the training of character as in cultural development. A measure of freedom was allowed in the planning and performance of fancy-dress dances, where the aristocratic young ladies were no doubt delighted to dress up as befitted their rank, for, although there was no school uniform, the nuns insisted on simplicity. With many of the senior pupils, there was evidently occasional need for the reading of school rules on these points. "Powder for the hair" was considered a necessity for a very long time, but until the ostentatious fashions of the eighteenth century toned down, the nuns were constantly waging war on dresses embroidered in gold and silver. A note in the State archives in Munich gives us this information.

In the boarding-schools the girls got up at 6 A.M. in summer, and 6:15 in winter. Mass at 7 A.M. was followed by break-fast. Then came lessons from 8 until 10:15, which was the dinner-hour. Recreation lasted till midday, after which there was French conversation for an hour; then lessons again until four, when there was refreshment, followed by recreation. At five the rosary was said; then there was a free period until supper at 6:30, again followed by recreation. At 8 the children went to bed. Thursday was more or less of a holiday every week, but the preparation of lessons for the next day was always exacted. Walks were allowed on Sundays and feast-days; and in summer a whole day in the country seems to have been the usual treat given to the children. Other holidays comprised a few days at Christmas and Easter, and three or four weeks in September; the hazards of travelling were such that the children never went home for holidays. Their parents visited them whenever they could, but they seem to have trusted completely in the motherly kindness of the nuns, who, on their side, saw to it that the children wrote home regularly. These letters were not read by anyone before they were posted, nor were the incoming letters from parents read by the nuns. One other point about the daily life in the boarding-schools: In the early days the boarders had to bring not only their bed linen, but mattresses and even the bedstead itself, exception being made for foreigners, who paid nine florins for curtains and linen and two florins for the wooden bedstead. The bed into which each boarder climbed, no matter how elegant she was, had a straw mattress covered by a feather-bed. The chronicle speaks of an "over feather-bed," presumably the seventeenth-century version of an eiderdown. There were, in addition, sheets, a bolster, two large pillows and a small pillow to put under the head. Complete silence was prescribed in the dormitories.

And how did a teaching nun keep up the demanding pace of mother, friend, counsellor, corrector of manners, teacher of Latin, corrector of exercises, while living her own deeply spiritual life? A sentence in the Diocesan Archives at Augsburg satisfies our curiosity. It tells us that Superiors were warned by Mary Ward to watch over the health of those employed in the schools: "They shall see to it that each one employed in teaching has one afternoon a week free so that she can take relaxation at home or in the country house belonging to the convent."

CARMELITE MONASTERY
Beckley Hill
Barre, Vt., 05641

DATE BORROWED